MW01687335

Jailhouse JUSTICE

Don Baron

Author, Canada's Great Grain Robbery

To John Schmidt!
With thanks!
Don Baron

THESE PEOPLE KNOW DON BARON

Read what people in the know say about the man and his book...

JAILHOUSE JUSTICE

"Jailhouse Justice documents one of Canada's best-kept and most shameful secrets: the Canadian Wheat Board's legal bullying of Canada's western farmers. Using startling real life examples ranging from pre-dawn raids to ominous high-level government "chill" orders, Don Baron demonstrates just how far the Wheat Board will go to maintain its oppressive monopoly on the Western grain economy. Like his earlier book on the Wheat Board, 'Canada's Great Grain Robbery,' Baron's Jailhouse Justice is required reading for anyone concerned about individual freedom in Canada." **Stephen Harper, President, National Citizens' Coalition**

"Jailhouse Justice tells the compelling story of a group of Prairie farmers fighting for the right to sell the grain they grow on their farms free of control by the Canadian Wheat Board. It is a story of individual rights and freedoms versus a state monopoly, of one's right to be in control of one's own destiny versus the right of the state to control an individual's economic and thus personal destiny. This book should be read by every Prairie farmer, politician and bureaucrat no matter which side of the issue he or she stands". **Verna Thompson, Publisher, The Press Review, Eston, SK, and President, Sask. Weekly Newspapers Assoc., 1998-2000**

"Don Baron chronicles in great detail Ottawa's aggressive prosecutions of idealistic prairie farmers who defied the Wheat Board monopoly as a political statement about property rights and free markets, and were jailed for their trouble. He also marshals abundant evidence showing that the CWB, whether by federal folly or malevolent design, repressed the natural development of the prairie economy. That such a monument to Soviet-style command and control economics survives in the 21st Century ought to shock Canadians out of their complacent faith in Liberal platitudes about our secure niche in the New Economy." **Paul Bunner, Alberta Report**

"Prairie historian Don Baron paints an accurate and detailed picture of the attacks on those brave souls who actually believe they have the right to sell the grain they grow. How silly of them. The fur trade monopoly of our Canadian roots has evolved to the grain monopoly of the Canadian Wheat Board. Jailhouse Justice is a chilling chapter in Prairie history. It's a must read for anyone who has an open mind and believes in allowing individuals to be paid for what they grow." **Joe Ralko, Author and former award-winning Canadian Press correspondent**

"Rarely do you get the whole story from newspaper clippings and television sound-bites. Don Baron's latest book goes behind the headlines and tells the story of how prairie producers challenged Ottawa's authority over grain marketing, and why farmers were prepared to go to jail in the struggle for marketing freedom." **Craig Docksteader, Coordinator, Prairie Centre/Centre for Prairie Agriculture**

"The true story is out at last. And what a mess we are in. The Prime Minister told students in the Ukraine the absolute truth – "Monopolies face poverty and stagnation. Monopolies are not worthy of a great nation and a great people. " But when Mr. Chretien returned home to Canada, he left his own wheat monopoly intact. That monopoly grinds down prairie farmers and the West itself. Could his message be more clear? He doesn't classify Westerners as a great people, nor Canada as a great nation.

"Farmers desperately need freedom to manage their farms and to create wealth. Their lack of freedom is killing small towns in the prairies. Yes. Saskatchewan grows the world's best durum wheat. But Mr. Chretien's monopoly won't let us have pasta plants here to process it. There are 14 pasta plants just south of the border, and Canada imports 84% of the pasta we use. We can't build Western Canada or in fact, Canada at all, until we end this nonsense, and regain our freedom to manage our farms and our businesses to create wealth and to build the West. **Clarence Taylor, Regina area grower and farm activist.**

"To farm in Western Canada is to live in the darkness of the CWB buying monopoly. A few of us worked very hard writing, speaking, organizing and yes, being incarcerated in order to throw gasoline on a smoldering problem. Don Baron has captured that story. This book will enlighten its readers and help lift this darkness over the West." **Jim Pallister, Pallister Farm Ltd. Portage La Prairie, MB**

"Don Baron has done it again. With a vivid writing style he has painted a picture that should make all of us shake our heads and wonder whether we live in a democracy or a dictatorship. When Jean Chretien's Liberals can put innocent farmers in shackles and toss them into jail for simply having the ingenuity to sell their own grain at the best possible price to customers they have found themselves, it is surely a condemnation of a rotten system. If our farmers can be frog-marched into jail in this way, what may happen to the rest of us when we invoke the Liberal establishment's ire? This is an issue for the World Court and the World Trade Organization to probe. Baron should be a hero to Canadian men and women." **Paul Jackson, Associate Editor, The Calgary Sun**

"**Jailhouse Justice** takes up the story of the administrative tyranny imposed on western grain farmers where **Canada's Great Grain Robbery** left off. No longer content merely to impose its bureaucratic fiat on the grain producing peasantry of Canada's west, the CWB has enlisted Canada Customs and the RCMP to imprison and humiliate farmers who dare to resist a compulsory but woefully inefficient monopoly. This may be typical behavior of tyrants everywhere, but it is still a shock to realize that these horror stories are enacted in Canada today." **Barry Cooper, Prof. Of Political Science, University of Calgary, and national newspaper columnist.**

"A blockbuster story!. The Wheat Board has Canada's largest public relations aggregation to tell its side of the story. Now, Don Baron has told the growers' side in detail for the first time in a way people will be able to understand. No wonder Wheat Board permit holders have dropped to 115,000 from a pre-war 250,000. Who would want to work under the stultifying conditions Baron describes? More to the point, Who's next in the farm sector to be saddled with an Ottawa monopoly? This book provides a long-missing service to Western Canada and hopefully to Canada." **John Schmidt , long-time reporter, columnist and author, including the Western Stock Growers' history, "An Experiment that Worked."**

"This remarkable story shines a fresh light on the astounding obstacles placed in the path of Prairie growers - not the constant and expected ones of weather, but the obstructionism of a formidable federal bureaucracy and its Wheat Board Monopoly. A reader is forced to ask, 'Why is the legislation imposed on prairie farmers different from that in the rest of Canada? Why must they be forced to sell their wheat and barley to Ottawa's monopoly while all other farmers are free to sell to the highest bidder?' The Wheat Board dictatorship and the Federal bureaucracy ensure that the farmer receives less than world price for his grain. Don Baron has unearthed the evidence - more and more Prairie growers 'want the freedom to sell their own wheat and barley to the highest bidder...(and)..to manage their own farms and business enterprises. They even want the freedom to get their grain processed in their home communities.' Obviously the Wheat Board and Ottawa see these 'wants' as undemocratic and un-Canadian, believe they must be stamped out even to throwing the farmers in jail. This story reveals the overweening power of an entrenched bureaucracy, and the farmers' desperate fight to rid themselves of this obstacle." **David Marshall, author of *Me and George*, the Canadian army's liberation of Holland from Nazi Germany**

"This book is must reading for all Canadians. It accurately documents the injustice western farmers have endured trying to market their grain. This mismanagement by government will in the end cost all Canadians. The story clearly demonstrates the CWB monopoly is not working for the benefit of growers. It prevents them from adding value to their crops, which is absolutely necessary for the economic well being of prairie agriculture. This book also reveals the tyranny Ottawa has stooped to in protecting this dinosaur grain monopoly." **Buck Spencer, Past. Pres., Western Barley Growers' Assoc.**

"Jailhouse Justice is a shocking expose of Ottawa's appalling Big Brother treatment of Prairie growers. Opposition MP's should take this book and raise absolute hell in the Commons. But lets not forget that a few farm organizations must accept some responsibility for this as well.. And look at the overall cost to Canada. I know from experience that Ottawa's 'Western' grain policy wrecked grain production in the Maritimes and it was also a major force in the explosion of corn production in Ontario and even more in Quebec. That policy also forced Central Canada's livestock industry to find alternatives to western feed grain and made the Maritimes even more the lackeys of Ottawa. Feed and railway policy, largely dictated by Ottawa, put Canada's livestock and meat industries at a disadvantage many times. And the Western livestock industry was disadvantaged for decades by the Crow rate. Some progress was made for the livestock and meat side, and also for oats, under Agminister Charlie Mayer. Yes, Jailhouse Justice tells a story all Canadians need to know of how shabbily their government and its creature the monopoly Wheat Board, can treat their fellow citizens." **Dave Adams, retired General Manager, Canadian Meat Council**

"Jailhouse Justice leaves no doubt, the monopoly wheat system is absurd. Why not set up a monopoly for all trees? When the trees are cut down, they must be sold through the Canadian Tree board. It will take delivery only if growers have a tree quota book and are asked to deliver to a saw-mill, a firewood lot, or to port for export. The Board will attempt to export all trees as logs so Canada will become a world class log exporter. Any foreign tree buyer will be offered these logs at a discount to the domestic lumber industry. Any lumberjack who tries to sell his own trees will have his chain-saw confiscated by Canada Customs, and the RCMP will handcuff him and throw him in jail alongside the wheat board convicts who tried to be entrepreneurs and market their own wheat. The simple answer? Let prairie wheat trade freely with a voluntary board, and stop fining and incarcerating farmers who want to market their own grain. Canada's natural comparative advantage will be fully realized and a heightened value-added industry will be added. If we allow it, wheat can become an even greater part of our future. More high value food additives will be wheat-based in the future. And wheat may one day become a major raw ingredient for industrial products – synthetic wood (i.e. fibreboard), a filler for the plastics industry and a further expansion of ethanol production." **Mark Hayhoe, President, Hayhoe Mills, Woodbridge, Ont.**

"Don Baron has done it again. Only in Canada can upstanding, responsible people go to jail for trying to make a better living, and in Canada only western grain farmers face that horrifying risk. This book shows the human-side impact of this ruthless, senseless, dictatorial system on its victims. This is the Canadian Gulag." **M.W. Dorosh, Editor/Publisher, Agriweek.**

Don Baron grabs the reader's interest in his first few sentences and his story doesn't relax its grip until the final paragraph. Starting with Andy McMechan who was arrested, shackled and jailed for 155 days for selling $300 worth of his own barley, Don documents case after case where prairie farmers have been treated like criminals for trying to market what they have grown without the questionable benefits of going through the wheat board. He focuses on both large and small government blunders, such as when a wheat board lawyer told the Manitoba Court of Appeal that the board's only mandate was "to dispose of grain in the best interests of the federal government as its agent. It has no obligation to obtain the best price for farmers." **Fred Cleverly, columnist, Winnipeg Free Press**

"The truth about the vicious choke chain that Ottawa holds around the neck of prairie farmers, and Ottawa's tactics in restricting freedom and wealth, has left me deeply embarrassed to be a Canadian. Don Baron has lifted the wool from my eyes, educated me to the shackles on these farmers and inspired me to fight back for freedom." **Craig Chandler, National President, Progressive Group for Independent Business**

Don Baron has done every Canadian a service by recording this story of the fight for the right to hold property that has been taken away by Federal government acts and by court judgements. The fight was not just a war of words, but a series of actions by bold and determined young men challenging unjust laws with loaded grain trucks. That's why this is a more vital book than Don's more comprehensive history, Canada's Great GRAIN Robbery. **Alf Bryan, grower, columnist, author of 'Katherine,' and other books, Tugaske, Sask.**

For nearly sixty years, the Canadian Wheat Board has operated behind a veil of secrecy. Like all totalitarian organizations, it knew that information about its operations would be its undoing. Knowledge in the wrong hands could be used as a weapon to destroy the monopoly. Don Baron has taken what he has learned about it to launch a scathing attack on its attempt to crush its opposition. This book will be required reading for those who wish to understand the West's struggle to end its colonial stat Canada. **Russell Larson, Grain grower, Outlook, Sask.**

PREFACE...

"It's time to bid adieu to the Wheat Board!"

This astounding story which goes to our country's heart, has been virtually unknown to Canadians. But by 1996 the national and prairie media were focusing on it at last. Thundered a Globe and Mail editorial, "It is high time Ottawa stopped treating the Prairies like a company town."

And columnists David Bercuson and Barry Cooper wrote, "It's time to bid adieu to the wheat board...both China and Russia are moving away from collectivism. Will Canada be the last country on earth to force its farmers to dispose of their produce as collective sellers at prices determined by bureaucrats?"

Yes, the truth is finally emerging about Ottawa's grain monopoly and raising perhaps the most important question in Canada today - Will Ottawa finally free up Westerners to return to wealth creation in the resources-rich prairies? Or will it continue to shamelessly impose its smothering political monopoly over the West?

An Edmonton Journal columnist described Ottawa's monopoly board as, "Marxism in action," added, "It...has nothing to do with farming and everything to do with economics and politics." The National Post cried out in June, '99, "Scrap the Wheat Board...one of the biggest obstacles to farmer prosperity on the prairies."

Editorialised the Globe and Mail in April, '97, "Let farmers do with wheat and barley as they already do with oats and canola: sell to whomever they want including the Canadian Wheat Board."

When Liberal Wheat Board Minister Ralph Goodale attacked the prestigious National Citizens' Coalition for supporting growers and called it a "voice of extremism," then Globe and Mail business editor Terrence Corcoran responded that freedom for prairie growers is a central issue in Canada today.

In a devastating appraisal of the monopoly's actions, Edmonton Journal columnist Lorne Gunter wrote, "The Wheat Board is Marxism in action...(it)...has nothing to do with farming and everything to do with economics and politics." He added, "I may not know feed barley from malting barley, but I know socialism when I see it. And the CWB is socialist pure and simple."

A Financial Post editorial in March., '99, weighed in

totally on the side of Chief Justice Willard Estey's just released study which urged the Liberal government to slash the CWB's tight grip on the industry. But The Post phrased it less delicately than did Estey. It urged Ottawa to get the "...command and control CWB butt out of transportation and leave the grain handling companies and railways responsible for getting grain to ports on time."

Estey had sensibly recommended "freeing up the overly-regulated, dysfunctional Western grain transportation system...Let free markets move the grain. And make the grain firms accountable to producers through binding arbitration. Make them compete through open tender for the CWB business and pay damages if the terms weren't met."

The Post editor said Estey was "...dead right in concluding the CWB should not have an operational role in transportation to ports...(for the board's) mandate already prevents farmers from freely marketing their crops as they see fit. There's no way the board should also have regulatory control over the allocation of grain cars."

National newspaper columnists **Bercuson and Cooper returned to this burning issue** in Feb., '99. "Liberals have long ignored the West," they wrote, "(yet the entire country pays) when more than nine million Canadians are seriously under-represented in cabinet and in the government caucus, for the Western viewpoint is lost in making major policy decisions."

They said the Liberal party "...has become no more a national party than any of the others.... It is a large regional rump...(and it has)...demonstrated a remarkable lack of respect for Western Canadians. Westerners have been treated like children who need to be protected from themselves and from the bogeyman of national fractionalization that haunts the consciousness of Ottawa mandarins."

Yes, some of Canada's most knowledgeable journalists and leaders have been crying out for an absolute revolution. And smaller prairie papers and other groups who see their own rural communities being devastated by these politics, are demanding action.

The Portage la Prairie, Man., paper reported in Feb., '97 that Can-Oats Milling was reaping the benefits of changes which had taken oats out of Board control. And its Vice President Karl Gerran said if Ottawa hadn't removed oats from the monopoly, his firm would likely have gone south.

Farmer-owned United Grain Growers' President Ted Allen argued in a Globe and Mail column in late '96, the need for a voluntary wheat board so growers could market their own grain if they so chose. And the member-funded National Citizens' Coalition announced in Feb. '97, a $30,000 media campaign urging prairie farmers to vote for freedom in an upcoming plebiscite and against the Wheat Board's monopoly on barley sales.

The Winnipeg Grain Exchange dipped a cautious toe into these roiling political waters with an advertisement focusing on the enormous price losses prairie growers were suffering. It said prices (in CDN funds) for equal quality wheat at Net, N.D., were $1.91 3/8 compared to $1.10 at Gretna, Man. And at Portal, ND, they were $1.87 5/8, vs. $1.07 1/2 at North Portal, Sask. Its list went on.

Journalists and others examining this struggle have written in terms of astonishment, outrage, bafflement, and dismay. And increasing numbers of Canadians say the price Canadians are paying for this flaw in our system is far too high – that remedial action can wait no longer. We can no longer continue to treat prairie people like second class citizens. And besides, this treasure house should be freed to become a main engine of Canada's growth.

ACKNOWLEDGMENTS

All Canada owes Dave Bryan and the numberless other growers in this story an enormous debt.

The tales of courage told in this book make it perhaps an unprecedented story. In their struggles to win freedom from the iron grip of Canada's biggest monopoly, these hundreds of growers won massive media coverage. They were filmed as their grain trucks were seized during their border crossings, and as they were arrested and shackled and hauled off to jail. These shocking events screamed out to the public in newspaper headlines and from TV screens and on radios across the nation. Editors of prairie community weekly papers devoted endless space to this human drama for a compelling reason. Those editors understood only too well the depth of this crisis. These growers were citizens at the very heart of their local communities, and they had lost their freedom to manage their own farms and to create wealth. Their farms were at risk and their entire communities were suffering – in fact, the future of the communities themselves were too often hanging by a thread.

I visited dozens of these growers in their farm homes, I sat in courtrooms as their agonizing trials dragged on, I watched as their wives and children wept at these catastrophic events. I will be forever in their debt for their patience as I asked them endless questions, trying to bring their stories into a clear perspective.

In truth, it is these growers themselves who have written this remarkable story. I have simply tried to faithfully record their struggles as they risked all trying to save their farms, their families, and the country itself. One thing is certain. All Canada owes these brave souls an enormous debt. But the story has only begun. Canadians must respond as well – they must bring pressure on an uncomprehending Ottawa government to finally free up prairie growers and the West itself, to get back to the business of creating wealth and helping build a strong country and a strong nation.

DEDICATION

This book is dedicated to my wife, Rene, who supported me at every turn during the endless hours as I wrote this book, and in fact, who has been my strongest supporter through our many years together. The demands on my time during a lifelong career as a journalist/author, meant that I too often neglected to give her the special attention that every wife deserves. And still, with her ever-smiling personality and her warm hospitality and her superb cooking, she welcomed and entertained the endless parade of friends and acquaintances I brought into our house. Perhaps too often, we wound up talking about my preoccupation – the events around us shaping every part of Canada, and particularly our agriculture and our food industries and our rural communities, and the personal struggles of the people involved. For these represented stories that I felt simply had to be told. But she unfailingly joined in those discussions with enthusiasm.

She deserves far more credit than she ever received. But I acknowledge that now.

A personal note from Don Baron...

YES, THAT SOCIAL GOSPEL CRIPPLED THE PRAIRIES...AND CANADA

My earlier book, Canada's Great GRAIN Robbery, was greeted by the media far too kindly. One writer generously began her review, "Don Baron...is a man with a mission – to bring (the prairies and Canada) the glory they deserve." Dozens, yes, hundreds, of other media people directed their audiences to it. I am grateful beyond words.

GRAIN Robbery was soon outselling Lady Di books and Stephen King fiction in some prairie bookstores. And it went across the country to Ottawa, Toronto, and beyond, triggering controversy and sales. It was short-listed for the Saskatchewan Book Awards.

In a brief introduction which I titled "That Holy Crusade Against Freedom" I went behind the scenes to explain what has gone wrong in the West – and Canada:

"...Walter Rauschenbusch and other Protestant pastors in the United States in the early 1900's were certain they had stumbled upon a new universal truth. 'Abolish capitalism!' they cried, labelling it and the open market the cause of human misery. Their preaching became known as the Social Gospel. It was scorned in the U.S. But when these pastors arrived in Canada, they were welcomed by Canadian pastors who soon joined in their crusade.

"When Canadian activist Salem Bland cried out, 'The distinctive task of the age is the abolition of capitalism,' he was applauded wildly. At a boisterous 1918 Winnipeg meeting, church and labour and socialist leaders stood and cheered the Bolshevik revolution.

"These pastors and those who joined them, were oblivious to one vital truth – competition and the free market are the very basis of personal freedom and wealth production. Canadian historian W.L. Morton has since labelled that Social Gospel a 'false doctrine.' But the social gospellers carried their holy crusade to the centre of Canada's politics in an all-out assault on capitalism and the free market. Yes, Canada's grain industry has been mired in politics almost from the beginning.

"The rhetoric surrounding these events has been so fierce that few Canadians have grasped the real issues. This book tells the dark story of how mistakes made in those early years went to Canada's heart at untold cost."

GRAIN Robbery reported for the first time research and insights that tell why the prairies has failed to fully develop its vast resources wealth. Saskatchewan with nearly half of Canada's fertile farmland and untold resources wealth has faltered badly indeed. Its population languishes at 1 million, little more than 60 years ago. Manitoba has similarly suffered.

Alberta's people rejected that social gospel, focused on wealth creation opportunities not shut off by that legacy. And its population has soared from 700,000 to 3 million. But make no mistake! Saskatchewan, Manitoba and even Alberta have enormous unused resources and potential.

As editor of the national agricultural magazine Country Guide for many years, I had the opportunity to travel Canada's rural areas visiting farms and attending farm and business and political meetings. When I was Head, CBC Agricultural and Resources TV, my producers filmed programs across the country which gained big prime time audiences. One reality kept leaping out - the West's vast potential!

But too much of it cannot be seized because of the social gospel legacy. Yes, the West has excellent schools and world class universities. But when the kids are educated and go looking for jobs, they too often must go elsewhere.

Alberta is in phenomenal growth because of its energy resources and because its people rejected the social gospel and welcomed the entrepreneurial spirit. If Ottawa, along with Saskatchewan and Manitoba had opened the door to that spirit across the west, the prairies would have turned massively to processing its enormous grain crops. "Value added," it's called. It means increasing the value dramatically of the raw crops grown in the prairie treasure house.

But Ottawa's policies forbade that. The Crow Rates, for example, subsidised raw grain shipments out of the prairies, but not processed products. This forced dozens of prairie flour mills to shut down, robbing the West of jobs and wealth creation, preventing a full-scale move into food processing and value-added. Ottawa's grain monopoly seizes every grower's wheat and barley as it comes out of the combine, denies him the freedom to sell it to waiting markets. It robs growers and the industry of the freedom to manage their own operations

No, the West doesn't process its grain into flour and breakfast cereal and bread and cakes any longer. Ottawa transfers the jobs and the wealth to Central Canada. The

West is reduced to importing its value-added products. It's the same with uranium and oil and gas. These resources are taken out of the ground, but too often, any further jobs go elsewhere.

Take one recent example. Prairie farmers grow most of the quality durum wheat harvested in the rich Canada/US prairie food basket. That durum is the basis of the fast-growing world pasta industry. But growers are not allowed to sell it. That durum is shipped out by Ottawa's monopoly to be processed elsewhere. Fourteen pasta plants are going all-out a few miles south of the Manitoba and Saskatchewan borders to meet the exploding demand. Canada imports 84% of the pasta it uses.

These prairies may be the richest 'undeveloped country' on earth - the one place where our entrepreneurs should be investing. But Ottawa's political stranglehold prevents them using their ingenuity to create jobs and wealth. That's why prairie towns are shrinking, the kids are leaving.

This calamitous story has been largely hidden from Canadians. But the truth is finally coming out. And one thing is certain. If Ottawa continues to strangle the West, the kids will continue to leave and the West to wither. To win back the freedom to build Canada's prairie treasure house, prairie people will have to wrestle the politicians for it.

Some myths remain to be exploded of course. One-time New Zealand Labour Minister Roger Douglas recalls that the government in which he served got that country's economy moving by abolishing privilege and giving power back to the people. Why did that work?

"You can't regulate a sick economy back to health!" he explained. "Command economies...(have been) tested to extinction. Governments are the most oppressive vested interest of all. Their role today is to create a framework that widens people's opportunities for choice, improves the incentives."

In the prairies, power may finally be returning to the people. And for good reason. Sixty percent of farmers attending the "Year 2000 University of Saskatchewan Seminars" in January said they were connected to the internet. Farmers who are smart enough to grow their crops are smart enough to market them. Free trade is transforming the world. An increasing torrent of products based on prairie resources is being sold to California and other states, and to Europe and Russia and the Orient and beyond.

But this is just the beginning. A vital part of the challenge ahead is told in this story, much of it for the first time.

A STORY OF HELL

When Andy McMechan walked into the Calgary Sun office in early 1997, Associate Editor Paul Jackson described what he heard as..."A story of hell reminiscent of human rights abuses in some third-rate South American banana republic and straight out of the gulags in the former Soviet Union...But it happened in Canada, and is so frightening, everyone of us should fear for our freedom."

"McMechan, a tall lanky Manitoba farmer was arrested, shackled, hauled into court and jailed 155 days..."

What was his despicable crime that earned him such wrath from the state? He had brazenly sold 50 bushels of his own waxy barley to a customer in the U.S. The barley was worth just $300. For this he endured that long incarceration and spent 47 days in the courts facing his interrogators and prosecutors.

"I would never have believed this kind of thing could happen in Canada," he told Jackson. "I'd never broken a single law in my life and here I was being hounded as if I were a criminal."

Wrote Jackson, "Not only was he jailed, but he was ordered to hand over his tractor to the federal government... How can a farmer farm without a tractor?"

Then Jackson added, "OK, the story is admittedly more complex than this, but the more you dig into it, the more horrific it becomes.

"McMechan, a father of four, is one of some 100 Western Canadian farmers facing widespread charges because they failed to hand over their wheat or barley to the Canadian Wheat Board, which operates as middleman.

"Under federal law, Western farmers are not allowed to find their own markets or customers for what they produce and legally own. Strangely the law does not apply to farmers in Ontario or Quebec.

"Western farmers have increasingly been fighting Ottawa's domination, and the Alberta government is siding with them against the wheat board."

"McMechan, now a folk hero among farmers and free enterprise groups, farms 960 acres in Man. and 640 acres in North Dakota. When he approached the wheat board about selling his harvest of waxy barley he was told there was no market for it. Simply put, he proved them wrong."

Don Baron, 14 Wood Crescent,
Regina, Saskatchewan, Canada
S4S 6J7
Ph./fax 1-306-586-4578

Canadian Cataloguing in Publication Data

Baron, Don, 1927-

JAILHOUSE JUSTICE

ISBN 0-9696913-1-9

1. Grain Trade – Prairie Provinces
2. Politics – Canada
3. Agriculture and state

Cover Design by
Leo C. Peters, The Creativity Coach

ORACLE HOUSE
Calgary, Alberta

Printed and bound in Canada by Friesen Corp.

CONTENTS

1

Farmer Tossed Into Jail Cell With Two Accused Murderers, An Armed Robber

For decades, Ottawa has been denying Andy McMechan and all prairie growers the freedom to sell the grain they harvest each fall. Instead, its monopoly board seizes their wheat and barley at prices below world levels. To fight off bankruptcy, desperate growers began hauling their grain to beckoning U.S. markets in the early '90's, pocketing the cash and returning to pay their bills. McMechan and dozens of others were arrested, shackled, strip-searched and jailed.

ANDY MCMECHAN'S NAME BLAZES ACROSS PRAIRIES AND INTO OTTAWA

The squeeze of low grain prices was tightening like a noose around the neck of every prairie grower in the early 1990's. And in their desperate search for relief, a few of them spotted a glimmer of hope. It was like the early morning sun peeking over the eastern horizon on a clear summer day. Buyers in the nearby US were paying prices to their growers that seemed too good to be true, for grain similar to that grown in Canada. And those buyers were eager to get Canadian grain as well.

But if Manitoba grower Andy McMechan or his neighbours wanted to cash in on those prices, Ottawa's monopoly board blocked the way. Andy's grain was in his own bins. It had never left his farm. But he was denied the freedom to get those top prices, forced instead to deliver his wheat and barley to the government Wheat Board. And in those days, the prices it paid were pitiful indeed.

"Ottawa's board compelled me to buy my own grain back from the board in a 'buy-back' procedure before it would give me a permit to haul it to the US for sale," he explained. Yes, he would have to buy his own wheat before he could sell it.

Here surely was bureaucracy running wild. "It doesn't make sense for me to have to buy something I already own," said Andy.

But he and countless others were becoming desperate for revenue to pay their bills and keep farming. Some of them finally decided they had no choice. They began to ignore Ottawa's "buy-back" and to haul their grain across to those waiting buyers. Then they pocketed the bigger cheques and returned home to pay their bills.

What happened next is perhaps one of the most disturbing stories in Canada's history. Ottawa decided these growers were riding roughshod over Canadian law. And it acted. McMechan and dozens of others were arrested for their desperate crimes. But it was McMechan who was targeted by Ottawa as an example who could be paraded as a law-breaker and a criminal.

The media now began to report these strange happenings and McMechan's name blazed into the news more brightly than all the others. By February, 1997, his picture was on the cover of the prestigious Financial Post magazine along with a seven-page story of his ordeal. It told how he was tossed into a jail cell with two men charged with murder and one with armed robbery. He was paraded in chains and leg irons and strip searched more than 50 times. And he suffered a multitude of other costly indignities. He was held in jail for 155 days.

Yes, this Manitoba grower's story was being shouted out across the country and stamped indelibly into the minds of Canadians. He and dozens of other growers were paying the price for hauling wheat and barley they grew on their own farms across the U.S. border to get those higher prices.

But was Andy being seen by Canadians as a villain? Or as a hero? That's what this story is about.

COWBOY ICONS – THAT FAMOUS WAXY BARLEY

McMechan and his wife Pam are prairie farmers and devoted family people. In a sense, they are cowboy icons–usually dressed in cowboy boots and denims and shirts. Andy stands a lean 6'2". His hair is often uncut, hanging long and curly. His voice has a rich deep resonance. He can be deadly quiet at times. But not from timidity.

The McMechan farm straddles the Canada/US Border. He and Pam kept 250 head of cattle on their US land as a second enterprise to earn vitally needed extra revenue. But when he was jailed, he had to give this up.

McMechan had first rebelled against Canadian Wheat Board regulations in 1993. He and fellow Manitoba grower Bill Cairns were charged in Dec. '94, with four counts of failing to provide export permits to a Customs officer, for 96 loads of grain trucked to the US in '93 and '94. A judge stayed the charges. But he administered a costly sentence ordering Andy to keep the peace, to have no contact with customs officers and not to leave Manitoba except to go to his own US farm.

But how could any grain grower/cattleman/businessman survive such restrictions?

In the summer of 1995, McMechan grew 20,000 bushels of a specialty waxy-type barley. It would be worth twice as much as regular barley if he could sell it for human food. But when he asked Ottawa's monopoly board about marketing it, he got back a brusque reply. The monopoly lacked any plan to sell this special barley as human food.

"Sell it through regular markets," he was told. And that meant delivering it to the board as ordinary grain at low prices. Yet he knew from bitter experience the only way to get that extra money for the extra quality would be to deliver it to the US. This left him with another agonising, perhaps even fateful, choice. The long-festering dispute over government grain marketing was bursting into the media in the summer of 1995, setting off a conflagration that is burning fiercely even today.

That dispute saw Ottawa's monopoly and Ottawa's Liberal government together with left wing farm groups lined up on one side of the struggle. Arrayed against them were growers who saw farming and food production as a serious business that should be kept largely free of politics. These business farmers wanted to roll up their sleeves and use every bit of energy and ingenuity and the explosion of technology to create wealth and generate more revenues.

They also wanted the freedom to market it themselves to the highest bidders. And increasingly they wanted to lead the way in having it processed in their own communities into value-added food products like flour and pasta and pastry and livestock feed and meat. And then to see it sold across Canada and into fast-growing world markets. This would create wealth and jobs and build their own towns and cities.

If McMechan now stepped back from this challenge and submitted to Ottawa's political will and to its all-powerful board, he would get less than $3 per bushel. His revenue loss would exceed $50,000. It would probably cost him his farm. But he might escape an excruciating struggle with Canada's justice system.

If he turned his back on Ottawa's monopoly and trucked his waxy grain to eager US buyers, he would get $6 per bushel. He would be able to pay his bills and keep farming. For Andy and Pam, farming was their life. But in the eyes of the governing Liberals, he would have broken the law. He would also be challenging Ottawa's iron grip on prairie grain - and its political hold on the West itself. He might even face months or years of legal struggle and enormous legal bills. And perhaps jail.

THAT FATEFUL BORDER CHALLENGE - JAILED, PITCHED INTO THE PUBLIC SPOTLIGHT

Despite that fearful possibility, Andy felt he had no choice. He joined a cross-border convoy of growers in late 1995, pocketed $6 per bushel for his grain, then headed home to pay his farm costs, buy groceries for his family and educate his kids, as well as to support his local community and build Canada.

But on reaching the Canadian border he was arrested. And this pitched him into the national spotlight. His story caught the public's imagination as seldom happens, and he was soon at the centre of furious heated debates in Parliament. He quickly became a hero, perhaps a martyr, his name a household word across the West and beyond. He had become the symbol for this long-simmering political dispute.

In fact, this quiet farmer became the quarterback who kicked off a struggle that rages in Canada today. For while the Ottawa board refused to buy his waxy barley, it dominates the prairie grain scene by enforcing its monopoly with an unyielding hand. Yes, Ottawa's will is imposed rigidly through this board and through Canada Customs too. And the courts. Growers must adhere to Ottawa's rules. And these are among the strangest rules outside of old communist Russia.

The most curious one deems that growers don't normally own the wheat and barley they grow on their own farms if they want to sell it. Instead Ottawa seizes control of that grain while it is still in their bins.

Growers who want to sell it out of province, or for export or for processing, must first do a "buy-back," in which the board sets a price which it must be paid. And the rules say no one can dispute that price. Growers know that the buy-back price will be so high they will make no money.

This "lack of freedom" issue goes to the very heart of the prairies. And in the early 1990's it was a simmering dispute coming to the boil. McMechan's arrest signalled a new phase in the struggle. An emerging new generation of prairie farm leaders - people who were pillars of their own rural communities - rallied to his support. They would stand with him.

IN A JAIL CELL WITH TWO ACCUSED MURDERERS, AN ACCUSED ARMED ROBBER

Hours after his arrest, the news was out that he was in maximum security at Brandon Correctional Institute, and his supporters believed this action could not have been taken without support from high political circles. And it seemed the Justice Department had abandoned any sense of reason or compassion. Unbelievably, this good family man was locked in a jail cell with two accused murderers and an accused armed robber.

One McMechan supporter wrote to Justice Minister Allan Rock that the monopoly by its own admission, had "no real commercial market for this waxy barley...Yet when McMechan found a lucrative market in the US and hauled there, they jailed him. Why did they do that?" he asked.

He said the market McMechan had found for his waxy barley was vital to him to save his farm and his family's place in the community. It would enable him to settle his outstanding commitments to the government lending agency, the Farm Credit Corporation.

Justice Minister Rock ignored his plea. It was a grim start. But McMechan's trial lay ahead, so he would soon be out of jail and facing the ordeal of preparing for it.

Dave Sawatzky was another of those prairie growers who was desperate for cash to pay his bills. And he also succumbed to the temptation of those high market-based

US grain prices. Sawatsky was a 32-year old church-going family man who had begun fighting back in the early 1990's against the monopoly Board's tightening grip. His growing need for cash on his Gladstone, Man., farm and his simmering exasperation with the monopoly's rules prompted him to begin hauling to the US.

He started with grain from his own farm, then began hauling for friends and neighbours and returning with their needed cash. He was soon being offered more grain by grateful growers than he could handle going day and night.

He hired other trucks and moved about 600 truckloads in 1993 and '94, crossing at Manitoba border points. At times he was buying grain from farmers and hauling it. Some observers say now that at least a dozen farm families would have lost their farms without Sawatsky's efforts. To say nothing of his own farm. His initiatives are said to have also saved Manitoba Crop Insurance and the government's Gross Revenue Insurance Program hundreds of thousands of dollars from crop loss claims.

Sawatzky hauled 880 loads before he was finally stopped and jailed. Looking back later, he observed, "Growers needed cash desperately. The wheat board seemed to have no idea what to do in this crisis. The industry clearly requires more options. Growers need freedom to market anywhere with no government strings attached."

When Sawatzky's case first came up in early 1995, wheat board chief Lorne Hehn seemed to almost wash his hands of the affair, issuing a curt press release, "Nothing we (CWB) can do about it."

Hard-pressed growers saw this as a sign of hope. The lack of freedom to sell their own grain was a life or death issue for their farms. But now the monopoly took another look at that gathering storm of discontent. It began to devise a furious response.

As the Crown built its case against Sawatzky and others, the growers reported more sinister events. "The police got search warrants and ransacked the houses of growers," said one news release. It was the beginning of an unbelievable period in Canada's history.

The Crown's alleged charges against Sawatsky and other growers were reported starkly by a growers' group in a Dec. 7th, 1995 news release. "Mr. David Sawatzky did between Nov 30, 1993 and Aug 12, 1994, at or near the customs ports of Boissevain, Winkler, Gretna and Emerson-West Lynne, in Man., fail to provide a wheat board license to customs officer..."

By then, Canada Customs had laid about 100 similar charges against growers. But this Sawatzky case was destined to set the stage for dozens of others that would later hit the courts and would drag on endlessly. The costs to growers themselves and to taxpayers and the country would be excruciating. All because farmers wanted to sell what they grew.

SAWATSKY'S ACQUITTAL RESONATES MESSAGE - BOARD PERMIT NOT NEEDED!

Sawatzky represented himself in court, and he stated the issue clearly: "The Wheat board monopoly is what is at issue here. It's totally, totally against freedom and democracy."

News reports informed the public of the ongoing drama. A Canadian Press/Regina Leader Post story Nov. 17, '95, reported that Sawatzky received a setback when a judge ruled charges of illegally exporting grain were valid.

Another CP story soon reported, "Sawatzky has admitted he has exported wheat and barley to the US on 860 occasions without a licence." As the case came to its climax, half a dozen growers had driven their huge grain trucks to Winnipeg in a show of support. And they jammed those semis onto a side street outside the courthouse. Other Sawatzky supporters crowded into a small courtroom.

The Winnipeg Sun did a telephone poll and reported 78% of those answering said these growers should defy the law in their battle with the monopoly board.

The trial was temporarily side-tracked when the Crown brought in the French version of the Customs Act. Sawatzky argued he wasn't charged in French, didn't speak French, and the court should use the English version. As the judge mulled this question, dozens of farmers milled about outside the packed courtroom.

The Sawatsky trial ended Dec. 4, '95. A verdict would follow soon. A group of fellow farmers who were outraged at Ottawa's aggressive and high profile pursuit of Sawatsky, fought back in the only way they knew, reporting, "Over 100 farmers are now standing up for their right to export their grain, and are facing fines."

Finally on May 17, 1996, Provincial Court Judge Arnold Conner's ruling on the Sawatzky case came down. And it resonated across the prairies and exploded into Ottawa's political circles.

No, said the Judge, a wheat board permit wasn't required after all. No law had been broken. The Customs Act did not require an exporter to provide customs officers with a permit to take grain across the border.

Dave Sawatzky was acquitted. By implication, the other growers who were charged must now be innocent.

Surely a historic ruling! If it stood, growers had at last won their freedom to manage their own farms and to sell the grain they grew themselves to the highest bidder. This could change the destiny of the prairies and even of Canada.

But even then, other momentous events were unfolding.

GOODALE JUMPS TO TIGHTEN OTTAWA'S GRIP

Sawatzky's acquittal, along with an increasing tide of border-crossings by grower caravans, confronted Wheat Board Minister Ralph Goodale with decision time. This Regina MP left no doubt he had no intention of admitting defeat - of allowing so many prairie growers their long sought freedom to market their own wheat and barley.

Within minutes of the Sawatzky ruling, reported farmers, Goodale rushed an order-in-council through cabinet to "strengthen and clarify the regulations." It required anyone exporting wheat or barley from Canada to give Canada Customs officers at the export point, the export licence for that specific shipment.

Grower Herb Axton of Minton, Sask., who was now caught up in this struggle, answered in a news release of his own. "Over the past two years, federal agmin Goodale has been accusing Western farmers of illegal activities. In the wake of this court decision, Goodale wasted no time." He saw that the Canadian Customs Act was changed, and thus, "...as much as admitted his department and the CWB knew all along that the farmers weren't doing anything illegal."

ONE OF THE STRANGEST BATTLES IN CANADA'S HISTORY RAGES

A furious battle was now inevitable. The monopoly Wheat Board was this country's major remaining crown corporation. It was backed fully by the politicians in Canada's "natural governing party" the Liberals, as well as the entire might of the government of Canada. And increasing numbers of prairie farmers now believed it was gearing for war against them.

That case was destined to have an amazing outcome. The besieged farmers refused to be intimidated and to buckle to Ottawa's will. They wanted justice and were prepared to throw everything into the struggle. Better to live in freedom, they believed, than to languish in chains.

And Ottawa soon began to see signs that the massive age-old support among growers for its monopoly was beginning to crumble - that old board supporters were jumping ship. It hadn't before come up against such a co-ordinated fury as began to emerge from those seemingly weak and forlorn growers.

As the days ahead would show, an anxious Ottawa responded by launching a massive assault on those growers using the fearsome weapons of alienation, humiliation and intimidation.

ONLY ONE DRAWBACK – POLITICS REIGN SUPREME

There may be no more fertile land out-of-doors than that which Bob Nunweiler crops near Rosetown, Sask. It has only one drawback. Its in the heart of the prairies where politics reign supreme over the market place, and bureaucrats seem to be forever in the way of rational decision-making. The resulting frustration has shaped Nunweiler's approach to every issue over the years.

Nunweiler is a mild-mannered farmer. But the burning curiosity he can never totally conceal sees him incessantly asking questions. He doesn't take orders easily without good reason. He can't abide bureaucrats who constantly give orders without accepting responsibility.

He was now caught at the very heart of a revolution gripping prairie grain marketing, and the industry itself. Nunweiler has been growing and marketing grain since he was a youth. And looking back over his years of frustration, he recently recalled, "Since 1965 I had personally witnessed what looked like a corrupt, inefficient and bureaucratic CWB being forced on farmers. I had written countless letters to the board, to politicians and to grain companies with no benefit. I had joined the Western Canadian Wheat Growers in 1975 to fight for my right to market my own grain."

This grower/businessman has fought endlessly for the freedom to become an entrepreneur in an industry caught up in breathtaking change. Yet he couldn't have dreamed the struggle would be so long and hard. Nor how costly it would be not only for growers, but for the entire country.

He recalls how grain was piling up on every grower's farm over a decade ago and the desperate financial problems that resulted. "In the years leading up to 1988, the monopoly board was selling only two thirds of our annual harvest," he remembers. And even then, impatient growers who recognised the prairie breadbasket's enormous potential were meeting and planning.

For decades prairie growers had been forced to produce raw products like grain and ship them to distant markets like Ontario and Quebec and overseas to be processed into value-added products. They were denied the freedom to have them processed in the West. The jobs and the wealth were created, not in the West, but far away.

"Not a great way," said growers, "to get the kids to take over the family farm."

Nunweiler knew well that the prairies were once dotted with dozens of flourmills. This was a way to add value to that grain – to boost farm income and to create local jobs. He was certain the prairies had to return to this 'value-added' industry. And he was prepared to help lead the way.

FEW HOSANNAS FOR NEW FLOUR MILL INITIATIVE

"With our grain pile-up, our family had no choice but to act," he recalled later. His dad Reinhold, and two neighbouring families acquired a facility remaining from a radar base shutdown at nearby Alsask. They installed a mill to process their own wheat, and began offering whole grain flour for sale.

No one in Saskatchewan wanted to try that Saskatchewan flour. Then they made a breakthrough, began to make flour sales to a market in British Columbia. This entrepreneurial coup cried out for celebration. Here was desperately needed leadership to the entire grain industry by one farm family. Hosannas should have echoed from every part of the industry and the West.

But the roots of Ottawa's monopoly board are anchored firmly in that ancient Social Gospel and its hatred of capitalism and the free market way. Too many groups still believed, "If I can't have it, nobody should have it." And this strengthened Ottawa's grip. The board's subservience to its political masters was only too visible. Its response to Nunweiler's initiative was not hosannas, but vilification.

"Its reward to us for finding this new market," he recalls, "was to send its officials to visit our customers and label us lawbreakers. They damned us because we weren't selling our wheat through the government board.

"It was rotten behaviour by government officials. It hurt our business and cost us many potential customers."

Unbelievably, Ottawa's bureaucrats seemed to be doing everything in their power to prevent a prairie taxpayer from succeeding in a business venture to create value-added with his home-grown grain. But Nunweiler refused to buckle. If he had to fight his own government which was attacking him using tax money it took from him, so be it.

Nunweiler's lawyer had written the wheat board at the start informing it of their plans. The board responded that the Nunweilers would have to haul their grain to a local elevator, then buy it back at the Lakehead price, paying the freight both ways.

"That was clearly absurd," recalls Bob, "Didn't make any sense at all. So we ignored the idea."

"Months later, wheat board inspectors began trying to enter our premises. Our manager would phone me when they appeared, and I told him to keep them out. I simply refused them entry. The inspectors gave up trying to go into my plant and began visiting our customers in BC, trying to get them to stop taking our flour.

"Meanwhile, we had been continually writing our MP in Ottawa, and I wrote again, said if the Ottawa monopoly wanted to do something, it should come directly to us. But to stop going to our customers. They finally backed off when I got involved in the new Farmers For Justice group."

Bob Nunweiler's brother Ross had experience in wholesale marketing, and he now became involved. They began making a pancake mix. And this product is doing well.

"We grow the best wheat in the world here," says Bob. "We should process it and sell it aggressively in every possible market. But the uncertainty is too great. Ottawa clearly wants to shut us down. So we hesitate to invest more and to go for all out expansion."

He admits the monopoly made a minor concession in early '96 after the growers' Moosomin border crossing, allowing farmer-owned facilities to grind their own grain as long as they sold it in Canada. But exports of flour and any other products were prohibited.

Nunweiler never has been a quitter. "Now we distribute our flour and mixes to countless consumers on the prairies, in BC and in the US Northwest."

He is one of those leading the way to a new era for the prairies and for Canada, even though Ottawa is using his own tax money to undermine his progress and impede his way.

2

HISTORIC BIRTH OF "FARMERS FOR JUSTICE"

Ottawa's monopoly board continued to stifle prairie economic growth as 1995 arrived, by denying growers the freedom to manage their farms and to sell their own grain. These farmers sensed the need for a new group to fight for their freedom, set out on a crusade to transform their industry and Canada itself.

TAKING ON CANADA'S BIGGEST MONOPOLY

One thing had become only too clear by the early 1990s. In a world of breathtaking change, the vital and priceless prairie grain industry was falling behind. Growers were experimenting with new miracle crops including genetically modified ones created by scientists to withstand diseases and drought and surplus rain. They were applying a dazzling array of herbicides to control weeds, and were powering their fieldwork with tractors bristling with the latest in technology. Their weed sprayers carried devices to read satellite signals from a U.S. government positioning system, keeping them on path within inches as they travelled up and down their mile-long fields. They might even wheel out quarter-million-dollar combines at harvest time.

These leading edge growers were ravenous for information, often travelling to meetings across the West and beyond, talking to other growers and businessmen and scientists. Many were at the very centre of the information revolution. Word processors gave them access to the Internet where, they could watch the prices of their crops in local and world markets minute by minute. And they could find buyers at any time. They could also see the rich opportunities ahead.

Farming had become the heart of a complex and fast-changing food industry. The challenge was not to grow a crop of wheat or barley – but rather to select and grow the most profitable crops. And perhaps to find ways to process them right on the farm or in the local community creating jobs and wealth at home. And to sell those products into exploding but fiercely competitive world markets.

But to seize that shining future required one vital but elusive ingredient – freedom to manage their farms in response to beckoning but fast-changing markets.

A PASSION FOR FREEDOM – A FIERCE STRUGGLE LOOMED

More and more growers were recognising this need. But Ottawa's monopoly denied them that freedom. And this was costing each of them untold thousands of dollars, bankrupting some. It was also triggering political tensions that threatened to divide and perhaps destroy the country.

The mounting frustration of growers was drawing more and more of them together to seek answers. Perhaps 100 had already made the border runs and many had been charged and were preparing their defences for their looming court appearances. They sensed the impossibility of working with their political masters in Ottawa who directed that monopoly. And now they put their challenge into a sharper focus. A fierce political struggle loomed. Greater unity was imperative.

Two growers who often chatted about these challenges were Keith Lewis of Wawota, Sask., and Paul Orsak of Binscarth, Man. Lewis had been a key figure in developing the fast-expanding and vitally important prairie canola crop. He had been a founding supporter and long term director of the Canola Growers Assoc. He was a voracious reader with a memory like an elephant. And he brought his years of experience in farm organisations to the table in this new challenge.

Orsak was a relentless and tireless leader in the pioneering free enterprise Western Wheat Growers group. A highly personable grower, he was one to get the job done.

News of Manitoba grower Dave Sawatzky's court trial for selling his own grain to eager U.S. buyers now filled the media. And the West watched intently to see if he would be convicted for his heinous crime. Clearly the time was overdue for a new and serious look at prairie agriculture in this beckoning new world.

Recalled Lewis later, "We decided we had to start looking very critically at that wheat board monopoly. And we quickly found this was of growing concern to more and more growers.

"A bunch of us organised a few informal get-togethers using word of mouth to get out the message. We were convinced new leadership was needed, and we hoped it would emerge. We planned a meeting in conjunction with Saskatchewan Crop Production meetings in Saskatoon and we rented hotel space. Thirty growers came. All of them agreed we had better get busy.

"We then organised a meeting in Winnipeg, and another in Calgary which was attended by prominent barley grower Buck Spencer from Lethbridge and many others."

The McMechan situation soon exploded into the news headlines, as the media saw it as a vital prairie issue. Growers discussed it endlessly, and feelings of alienation were taking root among many of them. The time for action had arrived.

THAT FIRST MEETING AT MOOSOMIN – WHO WERE THOSE RENEGADES?

Jim Pallister's roots go deep into the rich black soil at Portage la Prairie, Man, where his family has farmed for five generations. He fills with pride thinking of the challenges they successfully faced, and their achievements and those of their neighbors. Jim has a degree in agricultural economics and he and wife Colleen were raising their four children on that farm.

These three growers, Lewis and Orsak and Pallister now decided, "Let's do something about this." As it turned out, Pallister was ready to devote almost every waking hour and all the unrelenting energies of his lean 6'6" body frame to this challenge. The goal was to regain for farmers their long-denied freedom.

A fellow grower who got to know Pallister well observed, "He was ideal for the job. He has a quick wit and a mind like a steel trap that brings churnings into the pit of a bureaucrat's stomach."

The decision was made to hold a public meeting in early 1995. It was set for the Armories Building at Moosomin in southeastern Saskatchewan. An agenda was set out, speakers invited, coffee laid on. Paul Orsak chaired it and more than 50 growers came. They turned out to be characters of a remarkable kind, and one by one, just about all of them stood up and offered their ideas. Here was desperately needed new blood coming onto the farm leadership scene.

Johan Leitgeb understood as few Canadians could what was at stake in this freedom struggle. His father had farmed in Nazi-occupied Austria when farmers were required to sell their grain to the state marketing agency. In those evil days, they were told this was for the greater good of all – a statement Johan suggested was somewhat similar to what the wheat board tells every grower today – "It's good for all producers."

But in Austria, those who didn't obey were imprisoned or sent to concentration camps.

In his search for some way around the stifling monopoly rules, Johan was moving in the same direction as Bob Nunweiler, trying to start a flour mill on his Elie, Man., farm. He wanted to grind his wheat and that of neighbours, providing a new value-added market for the grain piling up on their farms. But the monopoly's rules blocked his way. Johan shared his story with the others at that meeting.

Nunweiler also spoke there of his family's struggle to set up a flour mill. And Bill Kent of Kent Flour Mills at Virden, Man, joined in those discussions seeking ways around Ottawa's crippling rules.

Organic/specialty crop grower and processor John Husband from Wawota, Sask., made a presentation and joined in the discussions. The highly articulate Curtis Simms who farmed at MacGregor, Man., was there as well.

The growers who planned this historic meeting knew only too well that every prairie farmer was now in a leading edge industry where science and markets and politics change hour by hour, and where growers who fall behind pay dearly. Keeping abreast of happenings was vital, communications all-important.

These growers aimed to keep the local media informed so the entire community could share their plans and many join in. Every grower in southeast Saskatchewan tunes in daily to CJGX, Yorkton, at noon, to listen to Jack Dawes, a tireless newsman and a nosy relentless searcher for farm happenings. Dawes informs his radio audience of every item he can find. And he didn't miss this first-ever meeting to focus on the growers' need to break free from the past and find a new course for themselves and their communities.

The weekly *Moosomin World Spectator* also reported these critical events to its readers.

As it turned out, the planners of that meeting were learning fast. In earlier hastily arranged meetings, they had sometimes neglected to pass around the hat to pay for hotel rooms and coffee and lunches, and they got stuck with the bill. This time, farmers were reminded and they threw in money to cover expenses.

A NEW FARM GROUP TO BATTLE CANADA'S BIGGEST MONOPOLY

As the discussion heated up, one thing became clear to these brave and venturesome souls. They must be ready to battle the federal political establishment in Ottawa and in the West, which stood solidly behind that grain monopoly.

At meeting's end, in a shrewd bid for more media coverage, they notified the RCMP they were making a symbolic protest. And they marched down the TransCanada highway, each carrying a sack of flour or grain. They proceeded across the Manitoba/Saskatchewan border in defiance of the Wheat Board Act, and this surprising display – so totally out of character for serious business farmers – sent out a dramatic signal. It said a new cohesion was beginning to cement these growers together in their common cause. The old days when politicians and bureaucrats could say nice things to a few farmers here and there, and then ignore them, were ending. Growers were joining together in an unprecedented crusade to transform their industry and their future.

And they meant business. They were taking on Canada's biggest political/business monopoly – Ottawa's powerful monopoly that did billions of dollars of business each year. Those who had come, and others too, were about to turn tradition on its head. They began to send in money to finance this struggle. Donations of $1000, $2000, even $2500, poured in. They created a new farm group, Farmers for Justice, through which to wage their battle.

The impact of this little band of growers on future events was to be breathtaking indeed. Carol Husband, who became one of its most dedicated members and workers, observed later with a patient chuckle, "It has become a bloody magnet for characters."

NO OFFICE BUREAUCRACY – MEMBERS DO THE WORK

These renegades chose a unique structure for their new Farmers For Justice (FFJ). They absolutely refused to set up an office. Members themselves would do the work. Every dollar raised would be directed to the job at hand. They pooled their talents and resources.

Jim Pallister made out the first list of possible members. And growers from across the prairies began to flock to this new group – men and women who were deeply stamped with entrepreneurial talents. These were people used to coping with the day-to-day challenge of growing crops in that prairie climate. They were on the leading edge of the onrush of technology. Some now grew only non-wheat board crops that they could market without political interference. And now they were determined to regain their freedom and were intent on moving ever closer to the vital marketplace.

But these renegades needed a network so they could communicate instantly among themselves and with the media. Quiet-spoken but determined grower/flour miller Bob Nunweiler stepped forward, and working quietly in his farm office, he set up a whole fax network linking the names of everyone who had come into the group.

As they began to make news headlines, these growers were viewed by some cautious observers as radicals. But they soon demonstrated they were simply resolute guys prepared to do what it takes to save their farms and their communities and perhaps even their country.

A WHEAT MONOPOLY, A FUR MONOPOLY – WHAT'S THE DIFFERENCE?

Regina-area grower Norm Colhoun was one of those who quickly joined these freedom fighters. He and others made an astounding discovery when they glanced back a century and a half into the 1800's. This grain monopoly which ruled their farm businesses and their lives was simply a case of history repeating itself.

They explained this curious fact in a remarkable news release sent out under the name of their new Farmers For Justice. In earlier days in the west, they said, it wasn't an iron-fisted wheat board with its hated rules and orders that intruded on prairie entrepreneurs. No, the business of the great Northwest then was fur. And the Hudson's Bay Company was the monopoly that stood astride that fur industry, and was in a sense the Lord of all it surveyed. It dominated the lives of just about everyone in that vast Northwest.

History tells us the tough and resolute Scots who led that trading company were fiercely dedicated to its absolute control of fur trading, wrote Colhoun. Any trapper who dared to market furs without the company's blessing would soon feel its wrath. The company would make open searches and impose stiff fines and jail terms.

Increasingly frustrated trappers in those early years saw this arrogant monopoly as unfair and against their rights. But investigation found the company's charter was legally sound. Dissenters had little recourse.

AN OMEN FOR GRAIN?

What was the fate of that fur monopoly? The story is clear, wrote Colhoun. The company charged a Metis settler, Sayer, and three others in 1849 for illegal traffic in fur. But now, the Metis decided to fight back. They organised in a determined effort to either peacefully or by violence, prevent Sayer being convicted. On trial day, 500 or 600 armed persons gathered outside the court.

Sayer was found guilty of illegally trading fur. But as it turned out, this was not a resounding defeat. No penalty was imposed. Sayer was freed. And this ended the monopoly practice in fur. Settlers could trade fur without risking a penalty. The monopoly was soon abolished.

That 1995 FFJ news release simply reported the obvious – "This sounds remarkably like today's wheat board tactics against western farmers." In fact, looking back, one can see that those events had an eerie similarity to the ones prairie growers were battling 150 years later.

"But was the fur monopoly's fate an omen for today's prairie grain monopoly?" wondered Colhoun and the others who had penned that release.

AN INCREASING TIDE OF CROSSINGS AS GROWERS 'DOUBLE THEIR MONEY' – MEDIA STORIES HEAT UP THE COVERAGE

An increasing tide of border crossings was underway

in late 1995 as caravans of desperate growers trucked their grain south for those higher prices. And they consistently refused to bow to the costly "buy-back" which would rob them of any profit.

Norm Colhoun had already made several crossings from his Lumsden, Sask., farm, more than doubling the Wheat Board's initial price for his durum. He netted $8.40 Can., more than double the $3.50 he would get at the local elevators. Most Canadian taxpayers would have groaned if they had realised what was happening and thought they were obliged to make up the difference for growers who were losing a fortune.

By now the media was intrigued. Headlining a story, "Caravan of Discontent," on Sept. 13, '95, the Regina Leader-Post pictured a huge line-up of grain trucks, and described protest caravans of growers bypassing the monopoly and crossing the border.

A few weeks later FFJ reported that more and more farmers were exporting their grain "without involving the monopoly board." And Ottawa's bureaucrats were meeting them with "acts of harassment, intimidation and even extortion."

Customs officers were harassing them continually. So the growers announced a new initiative. Their trucks would carry tape recorders and/or video equipment. And FFJ would press criminal charges against Customs officials if necessary. The RCMP was being kept informed.

FARM YOUTH INTIMIDATED BY CUSTOMS

Jason Farr was driving a truckload of grain across the border at Portal, Sask., in Sept., '95. It came from his dad Barry's farm at Lewvan, Sask. Canada Customs hassled him for a couple of hours at the border and indicated they were seizing the truck. Jason phoned his dad who advised him that if the truck hadn't been seized in those two hours, he might as well proceed and sell the grain.

Jason drove to U.S. Customs and agents again hassled and even intimidated the youth. Again on the telephone, dad Barry advised Jason to just park the truck and lock it. Meanwhile, Canada Customs officers were advising Barry by phone they had seized the truck.

"I asked, 'If it is seized, how do I get it unseized?'" recalled Barry later. "They said pay a $2400 fine and you can go home."

A quietly seething Barry responded to the Canada Customs officer, "You know what we are doing is legal. But if we don't end this right now, I will be going down there myself and we will have more trouble. How do we pay the fine?"

"He said, 'Give me your VISA number.' I did."

Jason proceeded to sell the grain in the U.S., pocket the money and return home.

The Farrs never did find out how the $2400 fine was determined, or what gazetted information enabled Customs officers to levy it.

And recalls Barry, "Jason was also threatened with criminal charges, yet he was just exporting his own grain. He was really shaken up."

Growers Garry and Randy Krieger of Lang, Sask., were also trying to haul grain to those beckoning U.S. markets. They had their two grain trucks seized in early November and held for more than four hours by Canada Customs. But the trucks were released when the two growers agreed to return home.

WITH FREEDOM BEING LOST, WHO WOULD FIGHT FOR CANADA?

The weekly Mercury paper at Estevan, Sask., reported on Nov. 8, that 50 farmers had attended an FFJ rally the previous week at a local motor hotel. Prominent farm and industry leader Art Mainil had addressed the group, calling on Ottawa to free up growers to haul their own grain to the US.

A long-time farm leader and farm builder, Mainil farms at Benson, Sask. He was one of the 'radicals' who had led the way as a group of growers battled the grain bureaucracy and built their own inland grain terminal – the first such project in many years in the prairies. He pushed hard for it and the Weyburn Inland Terminal was built in the face of fierce opposition.

Now, Mainil wasn't about to back down to the Canadian Wheat Board.

He had delivered several loads of his own grain to North Dakota, and had a particularly difficult crossing at North Portal, Sask., on Nov. 2, '95. He said Ottawa was using the RCMP and Customs "... to enforce its illegal position on grain marketing," and he intended to pursue it further in court. Later Mainil said the battle had cost him $50,000 of his own money and many other growers had spent that much and more on their freedom struggles.

Mainil is convinced many Canadians have not yet recognised the vital importance of this freedom issue – that growers must continue their struggle. His views have been shaped strongly by what he considers unbelievable experiences of two neigbors/friends.

One of them recalled to Mainil his youth when he was full of idealism and pride in his country. When World War II began, he had lied and joined the army at age 17 to defend freedom. He was paid $1 a day to fight in that war, often in the front lines, for four years.

Says Mainil now, "In more recent times his idealism has been shattered. He told me that if he had known our country was coming to its current state, he wouldn't have fought that war for any money."

That neighbour said, "Freedom is lost to us farmers. Our country is going the way those European countries went before the war. And we are beginning to pay a terrible price."

The other neighbour and close friend who greatly influenced Mainil, had survived the Bolshevik revolution in Russia. He married at 18 years old, and he and his wife had four children. But he had been on the wrong side of that war. And soon police began coming to their farm and taking everything they had – a cow, a horse, whatever. Finally, all they had left was a horse and a cart.

What happened next was even more shocking, said Mainil. His neighbour recalled, "I said to my wife, 'Lets go to town. It can't be as bad there.'"

But it turned out to be worse. He managed to get out and come to Canada. But he had to leave his wife behind. She and the kids had a terrible time – lived on soup for seven years. He finally got them out.

This neighbour told Mainil time and again, "Canada is moving in the same direction as Russia did in those days. Freedom is being lost. And the price that must be paid for that loss of freedom will be too great."

"DEFIANT REVOLT"...SWEEPING ACROSS THE PRAIRIES

"Defiant revolt is sweeping across the Prairies...

alarming Ottawa officials and startling observers," editorialized the Globe and Mail on Nov. 18. It went on, "Grain farmers in Alberta, Saskatchewan and Manitoba are flocking across the border, selling their crops illegally and wilfully being arrested in acts of civil disobedience...The anger is all being vented over the CWB."

Stuart Leis was one of the growers caught up in this struggle. This Kamsack, Sask., grower had a compelling reason to be involved. These strange rules were costing him $150,000 a year in lost sales. He was among the hundreds of supporters of McMechan and of Bill Cairns. And now he was one of seven farmers who trucked loads of barley and wheat across the border without a permit.

When his truck was seized, he simply got back in and drove off. And he urged other growers to consider following his example. He wanted 50 growers to bring their grain trucks, "...have them seized by Customs, then take them back." This would be, "theft over $5,000" – an indictable offence punishable by jail time. But it would be "the biggest act of civil disobedience so far."

OBSCENE FARMER-PAID BENEFITS REMOVED

The Winnipeg Free Press reported in late November that the growing outcry was finally getting to the politicians. With the monopoly under a farmer microscope, Ottawa had quietly removed its obscene farmer-paid benefits of eight weeks of vacation time and severance packages of up to $290,000 for board employees – benefits the farmers had no legal right to even find out about or to dispute.

Days later an FFJ news release directed to growers who wanted to export their grain, listed six members they could call for guidance and advice. And fully aware of the need to win the battle for public support, it asked anyone with a story to tell of how farmers had been controlled or abused by the monopoly, to please send it along. And to also send their views on how a freer system would be better for Western Canada.

Jim Pallister and other Farmers For Justice members leading this campaign seemed to be endlessly on their cell phones, thus freeing their organisation of the expense of a central office. But the costs of its high-profile activities were still high. Membership fees of $500 or $1000 weren't enough. And many growers who were now determined to rid the west of that government monopoly and regain their freedom were putting in more.

Don Skoretz was another of those renegades. A Sunday school teacher in his hometown of Yorkton, Sask., he had worked on oil rigs and his wife was a busy community worker. They were raising a family of what everyone agreed were "good kids." And he had already been jailed for hauling his own grain in a border crossing.

Blake Kotylak and his father and brother operated a sizeable grain and cattle farm at Montmartre, Sask. And Blake had also been charged in a border run. He had been featured in a farm magazine, and was seen by many as in the forefront of new technology and farming practices. He was a community leader. And he wanted the freedom to fully manage his own farm.

Curtis Simms was another of those into this freedom struggle. And a few months later, this MacGregor, Man., grower and others would be pictured in the Winnipeg Free Press in a cavalcade motoring through Saskatchewan to express their opposition to a Western Grain Marketing Panel's report which they said, "...scared us."

MORE OUTSIDE SUPPORT – "THEY WHO GUN-RUN GRAIN ARE NOT CRIMINALS!"

Other high profile groups were now stepping forward to support these embattled growers. Canadian Taxpayers Federation President Jason Kenney, who would later turn to direct political action and be elected as a Reform MP, wrote to FFJ in Sept., '95. His simple message was – Yes, his group fully supported the growers' goal to end the board's dual function as both a regulatory and marketing agency. In fact, his group believed implicitly that monopolies were not in the best interest of consumers or producers, even if government-regulated.

Hard-hitting editor Morris Dorosh of Agriweek who undoubtedly understood the issues better than any other journalist, focused on this exploding story in his Nov 13th issue. He reported more and more growers were running the border with wheat and barley without CWB export permits. And he labelled the issue "economic liberty vs. economic subjugation."

He explained why "...an increasing number of quite ordinary western grain producers are risking the kind of legal trouble and savage excessive fines that no one risks except in defence of deeply and sincerely-held principles."

And he wrote, "They who gun-run grain are not criminals, they are not martyrs and they certainly are not opportunists bent on victimising their neighbours. They merely have the guts to defy unfair, oppressive and stupid regulations of an excessively powerful state authority. They are trying to defend a natural human right: to get maximum reward for their work."

3

MASS BORDER CROSSING MAKES HISTORY

In a giant protest to support Andy McMechan, the new Farmers For Justice called on growers to defy Ottawa's monopoly and "Join in a border crossing for early March, 1996." The resulting mass arrest was one of the most remarkable events in prairie history. A farmer/war veteran who was there said, "I never thought I'd see in Canada what I have seen today." The ensuing trials lifted the monopoly's curtain of secrecy, gave the public its first glimpse of how Ottawa maintains its iron grip over growers.

IN TWO COURTROOMS IN SAME BUILDING, SAME DAY

The media spotlight focused on the courthouse at Virden, Man., in January, '96, where the trials of Andy McMechan and fellow grower Bill Cairns, were underway. Both had been charged with failing to provide an export permit when trucking grain to the U.S. Cairns had been charged for 96 loads trucked in '93 and '94.

Growers who rallied to support them found those events "...now bordered on the bizarre and the insane." McMechan said the legal battle had already cost him $40,000. And his farm was suffering because of the legal bills and the jail time which forced him to abandon his 250-head cattle feeding enterprise in North Dakota.

Then those FFJ growers reported in a news release, "Unbelievably, (the McMechan case was) in two courtrooms in the same building, the same day. At 2.00 p.m. yesterday, March 4th...(he was) fighting... actions by the Farm Credit Corporation (a federal lending agency) while ...across the hall, the family was fighting the CWB attempt to use Customs to stop them from getting what their grain was really worth."

Yes, he was in one courtroom for not paying his debts, and in another for selling his grain to get enough money to pay his debts. Canada's vaunted justice system seemed to be at cross-purposes with itself. Or did this apparent confusion serve a devious purpose?

Those growers insisted the monopoly itself was really on trial, for the Crown had failed to provide them with an Order in Council prescribing how farmers could obtain those controversial export licences. "Somehow the CWB has managed to get regulations enforced without the mandatory gazetting. The CWB has been JUST DOING IT."

Charley Mayer who had been Wheat Board minister in the Mulroney government and who farmed at Carberry, Man., was an unexpected witness. And in his powerful testimony, he stated his experience as minister had convinced him, "...what had been going on for years with the board was not right." Later out of court, he admitted that he agreed with efforts to end the CWB monopoly over exports.

The public was now being caught up in this curious case. And 78% of callers to a Winnipeg Sun telephone poll sided with growers. Their message was, "Grain farmers should defy the law in their battle with the wheat board."

McMechan said in court, "I'm still looking to find…the intent of Parliament…"

Growers were now convinced a curious game was being played. The Wheat Board Act provided for punishment for those who broke its rules. But growers believed Ottawa's ruling politicians and key Board bureaucrats feared a public relations fiasco if growers were seen being punished for selling their own grain. So instead growers were being charged under the Customs Act (they could be jailed as well as fined under its provisions) rather than the Wheat Board Act under which they could only be fined.

But these growers still believed the Canadian people retained a sense of justice and would not deliberately deny them the freedom to sell grain they grew on their own farms – that if the public understood, it would insist on changing the law.

"Parliament cannot and would not create a law that forces citizens to sell their property, in this case grain, to the government and then to buy it back at a much higher price in order to get an export licence," they said. "That would be simple extortion. Rules of Parliament and Cabinet have evolved ever since the Magna Carta, to protect the people from the Crown."

"The bureaucrats don't have the authority in law, and can't get it. But they are putting themselves above our elected government and using all the power this puts at their disposal to dominate farmers."

Those growers could only shake their heads in contempt that Ottawa's politicians apparently took no steps to bring this assault on them to an end.

AN AWESOME CARAVAN, 39 GRAIN-LOADED TRUCKS CONVERGE, MOVE SOUTH

These Farmers For Justice growers now launched another initiative that would grab headlines across the West and beyond and become one of the most remarkable events in prairie history. They had already set up a fax network as a communications line for all supporters of the cause. And they turned to news releases and word of mouth by members in dozens of communities to send their message resonating across the prairies

"Join in a mass border crossing as a powerful show of support for McMechan, and a show of defiance against Ottawa's monopoly board," they urged.

"Stand up with brave people like Art Mainil, Bernie Brodziuk, Bob Shaw, Bob Nunweiler and Charlie Culbert," they challenged. And they said other growers who would join in that crossing included Conrad Johnson, Dale Forrester, Danny Schultz, Darrol and Sheldon Wallin, Dave Bryan, Dave Rutledge, David Bouchard, Dale Peterson, Delory and Brian Nestibo, Don Skoretz, Gerald Carlson, Greg McIntyre, Henry Kuhl, Herb Axton, John King, Den Severson, Marce and Norm Desrochers, Norm Colhoun, Rick Strankman, Rod Flaman, Russell Larson, Stuart Leis, Stu Scott, Terry Fazakas, Wylie Dixon, and more.

That roster was almost a "Who's Who" of leading prairie growers. The response was remarkable. Within days an army of freedom fighters was coming together and 39 grain-loaded trucks converged and moved southward in an awesome caravan. They were heading towards the crossing point of North Portal, Sask., and on to Bottineau, N.D., to help load an 85-car unit train there. They were supporting Andy and also seeking badly needed money to pay their bills and to keep their local communities viable.

But they knew only too well what might lie ahead. Prairie growers are world leaders at producing grain and food for the world's people. At home, they were tilling the rich soil, creating wealth, educating their kids and supporting their communities and churches. And they were paying taxes. They saw themselves as businessmen with the same rights as other citizens. Yes, pillars of their communities.

But when it came to selling their grain, experience had taught them a bitter lesson. They had been deprived of their rights and freedoms to manage their own farms, and they felt like serfs doing the politicians' bidding.

Now a beckoning North Dakota market held out fresh hope. And the determined growers in this caravan were prepared to challenge Ottawa's monopoly. The weather had turned windy and cold. The growers had agreed to stick together, vowing if one truck is seized, all are seized. Customs officials had been tipped off and seemed compelled to view them as desperate renegades and lawbreakers.

The growers crossed into the U.S. and first-timers found those high grain prices were not fairy tales. The malting barley price in North Dakota on that March day was $3.30 per bushel higher than the Canadian price, feed barley $2.20 higher.

FROM PILOTING A BILLIONAIRE'S JETS, TO BATTLING BUREAUCRATS

One trucker in that caravan was a youthful Lumsden, Sask., grower and entrepreneur who could already look back on a remarkable life of adventure and an enviable life-style. Norm Colhoun has an easy smile and an outgoing personality. When you meet him, you like him. He's a social creature who enjoys being with people, chatting and learning from them. His lively curiosity continually seems to ask, "What's going on? Can we not address this challenge together?"

He believes instinctively that people are good - and he is devastated if it turns out otherwise in his personal or business relationships.

Colhoun began his career as a young pilot, won the respect of most who knew him. A British billionaire who sponsored yacht races hired him. He moved to Rhode Island in the U.S. and was soon flying a jet just about everywhere, including overseas. In a real sense, he was savouring the life of the rich and the famous. In a moment of relaxation today, he might show you a picture of the mansion where he stayed on millionaires' row there.

But that was an earlier day. His home today is on a

farm a few miles north of Regina. He and his wife Laurie also run a crop spraying business out of a hangar at Regina airport. And in recent years, he has been fighting fiercely against his political masters in Ottawa at enormous personal cost and self-sacrifice.

AN EARLY RALLY/BORDER RUN

Ask him about this freedom fight and he'll answer, "Let me go back to the start. It was in the fall of '95. Word came out of a rally for growers in Minton, Sask. Talk was plentiful about it. I decided to look into it further, so I loaded grain into my truck and I set off. Growers there included Herb Axton, Bob Shaw, and Jim Wood who would soon become household names."

"I hadn't realised the undercurrent of discontent among farmers then. But what those growers said made sense to me. I gave them some money to support the cause. And I hauled grain across the border on our first run.

"We went to Fortuna, N.D., southwest of Estevan. When we reached the grain elevators and talked to the buyers, it was like hitting paydirt. We sold our wheat for 1 1/2 times what we would get from the Board.

"We were so excited we went to a pub, had a drink and celebrated. We chatted and began to talk about an entirely new future for our struggling grain businesses – perhaps even the hope of keeping another generation on our farms.

"When we were crossing into the U.S., I had told a border officer of our mission and had no trouble. But later that year, our government sent me a letter, an 'ascertained forfeiture,' which said something like, 'You have broken the law, and are under charge.'"

Colhoun had no choice so he appeared in court. "I pleaded not guilty. But I was asked to pay all this money piled up in fines. Of course, I could appeal. And I did. This appeal has been in the office of the Minister of Justice in Ottawa ever since."

MASS CONFUSION AT BORDER PILE-UP LASTS FULL DAY

When the 1996 rally was planned to support McMechan, Colhoun was one of the 39 truckers in the caravan. There were also growers with half ton trucks and others who were taking Andy's own grain from his Manitoba farm across to his North Dakota farm.

Colhoun remembers that Andy had grown waxy barley, and he had a letter from the CWB saying it wouldn't take his barley. But it told Andy he couldn't sell it in the United States either.

U.S. prices were about double what the board was then paying, and Colhoun had hauled a lot of durum to Fortuna, N.D., and other places. He had also got to know another grower well whose name would soon be blazing into the media headlines.

David and Karen Bryan farm at Central Butte, Sask. David had simply refused to bow down to this government board's wishes and had "illegally" hauled wheat across the border. Now he and Colhoun came together on this run to support McMechan. They crossed and overnighted at a hotel at Bottineau on March 11, and the next morning, decided to delay a bit so they wouldn't be the first in line at the border. They hit the border at about 10.00 a.m., but were first there anyway. Other trucks began piling in behind them.

Again this turned out to be a calamitous event. Border officials had orders to seize the first two trucks as the convoy returned to Canada. A classic showdown was imminent. Only one question remained – would justice prevail?

The RCMP informed Colhoun and Bryan, "We are seizing your trucks!" They placed stickers on each of them, but the other growers with their trucks were jamming up behind them. Parking space was lacking, so Customs and police faced another decision.

"Six cruiser cars were waiting at an intersection a half mile down the road," recalls Colhoun. "So the customs/police ordered us, 'Drive your trucks down there.' Our trucks were already technically seized so we weren't sure how we could get in and drive them away. But we had no choice but to obey those commands."

"The rest of the trucks followed us down to the intersection. We parked, and the police ordered us, 'Get into the back of the cruiser.'"

"The cruiser radio was on and we could hear the Customs people and the RCMP were in dispute on what to do with us. Yet they were seizing all the trucks and other vehicles. They didn't have enough police cars to hold all the drivers.

"Again they improvised, ordered some of us, 'You can stand out by the car. But you must touch the car, so you are technically correct.'"

SANDWICHES, GOODIES AND COFFEE – COURTESY THE LADIES

McMechan's farm straddled the border south of Lyleton, Man. And Colhoun recalled, "Everyone there knew when we would be returning from our run. The ladies had come together that morning to prepare. Now, led by Andy's wife Pam, they brought out a marvellous feed of sandwiches and goodies. We were hungry and we ate.

"The RCMP were trying to make sense out of this confusing pile-up. We had some sympathy for them – they were simply trying to follow orders of some higher-up. And they were hungry too. We invited them to join us for coffee and sandwiches.

"They seemed embarrassed and puzzled – twisted uncertainly on their feet. But they finally swallowed their pride and joined us.

"Meanwhile, the grain truckers who had followed us across the border without checking in, were turned around by the RCMP and sent back to go through Customs. When they returned, they were in the same boat as the rest of us.

"There were 39 big trucks plus a bunch of half tons which didn't really qualify – they couldn't stop the half tons," recalled Colhoun. "It turned out to be a long and frustrating day for all of us. We had begun arriving at 10.00 a.m., but Customs took till 4 or 5 p.m. to get its work done.

"Some growers were arrested, shackled and hauled off to jail. Others asked, 'Were our trucks legally seized? Do we growers have the right to get back into our own trucks and drive away?'

"The police finally made a decision – called a bunch of wreckers to pull the big trucks to their Customs compound at Brandon. This threatened growers with the catastrophic loss of their trucks.

"YOU'LL NEVER HAUL ANOTHER LOAD OF GRAIN FOR GROWERS!"

"One of those growers was Art Mainil of Benson, Sask.,

who fully understood that if growers stick together, they wield big power. With these wreckers preparing to haul away the growers' trucks, Mainil stepped forward.

Recalls Colhoun, "He told the truckers in all seriousness, 'If you guys haul away these trucks, you can be sure you will never haul another load of grain for farmers.' Those truckers had no doubt Mainil meant what he said, that this was no idle threat. They believed he could carry it out. And they took heed.

"They muttered that they had to go back home. And they disappeared.

Yes, Art Mainil took care of that problem for us brilliantly. So the police remained mired in difficulties."

GROWER/WAR VETERAN OUTRAGED AT OTTAWA'S ACTIONS

The stand-off lasted until dark. The oldest farmer driving in the convoy was a 74-year-old World War II veteran named Stu Scott from Radville, Sask. Scott had stayed on in Europe after the war for the cleanup, then he returned home to farm. Pictures taken during those terrible war days hang on his walls at home. He brought home items of Japanese and German money issued only for war purposes. These are priceless collectors' items and he keeps them as historic treasures.

But now he was outraged at this humiliating experience. And his words seemed to say it all. "When we put our lives on the line in Normandy, France and Holland, I never thought I'd ever see in Canada what I've seen today."

"As darkness neared," recalls Colhoun, "we truckers made what we thought would be a helpful suggestion. 'We will take our trucks peacefully in an orderly convoy to the compound in Portage.'

"The RCMP realised there might not be room for all of them in the compound, but this could at least ease their current crisis. They said, 'OK,' and allowed the convoy to drive them over."

Everyone knew these incidents were protests, not criminal acts. But in succeeding days, the growers were charged as common criminals. Their crime – illegally exporting their grain without a Wheat Board license. Meanwhile Customs and then the RCMP had seized the trucks of dozens of growers. Six days later, grower Jim Pallister noted, "39 farmers had agreed to appear in Virden court the following Friday. That would be three days before Judge Coppleman is due to rule on the Cairns/McMechan charges."

FLAMAN "ACCOSTED BY CUSTOMS OFFICERS."

Another grower in that historic border run supporting McMechan was a young family man who cropped the fertile land at Edenwold, Sask., a few miles north east of Regina. His name was Rod Flaman and only months earlier he was still unaware of the higher grain prices beckoning in the nearby U.S. market.

Then he met Norm Colhoun at an agricultural meeting. Colhoun had already made a crossing and he broke the good news about the extra money being paid. These growers were now promoting massive protest caravans as a way of exerting political pressure to win freedom to market their own grain. And Colhoun urged Flaman, "Phone Art Mainil about it. He's going to the U.S. soon."

That conversation pitched Flaman into the centre of this fierce struggle. He had joined a border run just before Christmas, '95, and delivered his grain to buyers in Minot, N.D. Some of the group went to other grain points.

"Coming back through Lyleton, Man., I was the first guy across the border," recalls Flaman. What happened next changed his life. "On that return crossing," he recalls, "I was accosted by Customs officers. It was an unforgettable experience.

"These officers were rude and militant. They said in a condescending way, 'This is your lucky day. You will just get a warning this time, so you won't have to spend Christmas in jail.'"

Flaman was astounded. "I had been paid more money for my grain in the U.S. than the Wheat Board would have given me. And now Canada Customs officers whose salaries are paid by taxpayers like me, were treating me like a crook. Rather than frightening me off, this made me mad. I decided right then to do it again. And again."

The bottom line was that Flaman wanted his freedom.

FROM THE OIL BUSINESS – TO FIGHTING THE GRAIN FREEDOM BATTLE

Flaman had grown up on the family farm near Edenwold.

On graduating from university, he got work in Alberta's oil business, later returned to Saskatchewan to the family farm. His South Valley Farm now consists of 1600 acres of land, some of it sloping gently down to a tributary that runs to the Qu'Appelle river a few miles away. His dad damned up that waterway 50 years ago to get water for irrigation.

He has the skills and the energy to help move prairie grain and agriculture into a leading edge high tech industry so it can remain a world leader. But now he has devised a cropping program in line with today's badly twisted market forces. He doesn't grow any wheat board crops because experience tells him that's a political game. Politicians make the key decisions and this won't return him market prices. He is determined to get his farm onto a business basis.

He grows a U.S. variety of feed wheat – a non-board wheat – as well as feed barley, rye, canola and oats. To cash in on that irrigation water, he grows strawberries, raspberries, and saskatoons in a U-pick enterprise for people who want to pick their own.

A GERMAN HERITAGE – WORK HARD, FORGET THE PAY

Like so many prairie growers, Flaman's heritage goes back to central Europe. His grandfather arrived from Germany/Austria, with his bare hands and a willingness to work relentlessly. He picked fruit in the Okanagan for a time. When he had enough money, he bought a truck, headed for the Alaska Highway and began hauling goods there. Finally, he returned to Saskatchewan and bought his Edenwold farm.

Flaman's mother's family were Germans from Russia. Rod chuckles, "Germans are guys who like to work hard, don't care so much what they get paid."

His dad planted endless rows of windbreak trees and shrubs. And he would go out in the blazing summer sun and hoe the weeds. His dad was tough, made sure Rod got the work ethic. As a boy, he was never allowed idleness.

But now Rod and 27 other growers were charged for that series of protests in the spring of '96. As it turned out, the resulting court cases were delayed again and again through '98 with fascinating results.

Meanwhile Rod and other growers began crossing again the next spring.

JAILED FOR 155 DAYS

The trial of Andy McMechan and Bill Cairns had finally ended and the two were convicted in late March, '96, of illegally shipping grain to the US without a CWB permit. McMechan was fined $20,000 to be paid to the Crown and another $55,693 to be paid to the CWB. But defiantly, he refused to bend.

Cairns meanwhile refused to pay a $2000 fine. The Winnipeg Free Press asked the only meaningful question about that decision. "Why did he choose jail?" Farmers For Justice issued a news release praising Cairns' "Determination, persistence and uncompromising principle. This is what the country needs more of."

This Cairns case now settled into legal wrangling and dropped from the front pages.

As the months went on, McMechan had yet to pay his fines, and he explained wryly, "When in doubt, do nothing. They can come and get my assets." But now his need for revenue became critical and his saga returned to the media. He again defied Ottawa's monopoly and in March, '96, hauled grain to the U.S. without an export licence. On his return to the border crossing, a Customs officer and three RCMP officers met him. His tractor was ordered confiscated. He refused to give it up.

The next day he and a neighbour hauled 1500 more bushels across the border to his farm in N.D. Again when he returned Customs and RCMP officers were waiting. Andy explained what happened next.

"I sat there for 15 minutes and no one came out, so I left and went home. About 9 p.m. that night I was arrested at home for theft over $5000, of my own tractor."

He was again charged in July, '96, for failing to return his tractor to customs officials. Two months later, he was fined another $13,000 and sentenced to four months for breaching the recognisance.

His sentence turned out to be truly remarkable. He spent from July 9 to Dec. 10 – 155 days – in jail in 1996. He also spent 47 days in court. And he was subjected to more than 50 body searches for drugs and contraband.

He explained, "All I did was sell my own grain."

"I'm just an ordinary farmer," he said. "I don't want to be anything else. The same goes for the guys who were on trial in Lethbridge and other guys like me who have gone to jail. We have wives and families and they've suffered too.

"I asked my wife in December when I was still in jail, to have our children write me a letter telling me what they wanted for Christmas. She later handed me a piece of paper from my seven-year old daughter. All she wanted for Christmas was 'My Dad!'"

But now the public had rallied with support that left the McMechan family almost speechless. "We emptied our mail box on Dec. 24 before Christmas. Mail isn't delivered on the 25th and 26th. On the 27th, 80 more letters and cards of support were there from farmers all over the country – Quebec, Toronto, Halifax - ..."

DOZENS OF RENEGADES CAUGHT TRYING TO SELL WHEAT FOR CASH

That frenzy of border crossings in 1996 landed dozens of other growers into the courts, and many into jail as well. They went on trial in Regina and across the prairies, fighting for the freedom to use their own resources and to begin fully using Canada's great prairie treasure house at last. They wanted to produce more raw products and get them processed right in the prairies, creating wealth and jobs.

"How else can we build our rural communities and the West itself?" they asked. The freedom and welfare of every Canadian was involved. But that monopoly board blocked the way. This was a painful tragedy playing itself out and their cases dragged on for the next three years.

But other growers from across the prairies were now reading the unending news stories of these events, and were joining their new farm group, FFJ. This prompted the group to rename it Canadian Farmers for Justice. And since many of these new members had been lifelong Board supporters, but had now decided the monopoly was the problem rather than the solution, the growers had good reason for optimism. They were gearing up for unrelenting battle. And their numbers would climb to over 800. Counting those supporters who didn't feel they could pay fees, they would go well over 1000.

4

PRE-DAWN POLICE RAID TERRORIZES FARM FAMILY

As the struggle descended to lunacy, an editor asked the only question that mattered – "Why are law-abiding citizens breaking the rules at great risk, cost? Why deny growers freedom when they vote for freedom?" Highway signs cry out, "Canada is the only country to jail growers for selling their own grain!"

MOUNTIES JAIL GROWERS, WRECK FARM TRUCK

The headline screamed out the astonishing news, "Farm Family Terrorized in Middle of the Night." And the news release went on, "Armed men entered the home of Norman and Edith Desrochers...very early in the morning of April 10th (1996).

"Edith was just home from the hospital after major surgery. The intruders marched across the kitchen floor and disconnected all the phones. The Desrochers could call no one for help. Yet other intruders were in their farmyard taking one of their trucks."

That Canadian Farmers For Justice release went on, "These were not gang members, not the Mafia, but five RCMP officers and 10 Canadian Customs employees. Mr. Desrochers had exported his own grain a few days earlier without permission from the Goodale Wheat Board. This permission would have cost him thousands of dollars because he is a Western farmer, but is free of charge to farmers outside the Wheat Board Area."

The word was soon out that this furious assault began in the 5:15 a.m. pre-dawn darkness. Mounties and Customs officials entered the farm home at Baldur, in south-west Manitoba, where the Desrochers had farmed for years and had raised daughters Coreen and Monica and sons Clayton and Jeffrey. The intruders came in without knocking, triggering a time of terror for the occupants.

One well-read and perceptive supporter of these growers soon reported an almost unheard-of twist – the Desrochers' search warrant had been altered to read, "By day or night."

Yes, this family had suffered the shocking and terrifying experience of a late night police raid on their home. That invasion and intimidation was carried out, said Farmers For Justice, because Norman had been involved earlier in challenges to the Board's tight grain monopoly. He and other growers had sold their own grain. And they were convinced the government board wanted farmers like them jailed.

A shocked Alex McWilliams who farmed nearby, added more details. "These officials had come with two 10-ton tow trucks and a warrant intending to seize two grain trucks they believed were loaded ready to join a convoy to North Dakota."

Events then unfolded badly for these freedom fighters and for taxpayers as well. One of the Desrochers' trucks being hauled away on that warm spring day got stuck tight in the muddy yard. A 10-wheeler loaded with barley was taken to the Emerson, Man., Customs compound. But that compound would soon be submerged in the Red River flood.

TERROR FAILS, FARMERS VICTORIOUS

How could anyone explain these strange goings-on? Darcy Yergens farmed at Estevan, across the Saskatchewan border from the Desrochers. He had been one of the first from that area to export grain. And within days of the attack on the Desrochers, he offered his views.

A convoy of farm trucks through the Estevan area and on to the border had been planned and announced for the following day. The attack on the Desrochers would seem to be a tactic to discourage that convoy. But the attack failed.

"Instead, the police raid made farmers more determined than ever to defeat something they knew was wrong...That midnight raid told a terrible story. The state monopoly in grain has been revealed to be truly evil."

Yes, despite those fear tactics, over 50 farmers exported grain and returned home safely with their trucks. And with that success, another FFJ news release returned triumphantly to the Desrochers story, proclaiming, "Terror a complete failure, farmers victorious in Estevan."

But that raid of terror was costly for the Desrochers family and for the taxpayers too. Four months later when Norm paid to have his truck released, his barley had disappeared. He drove away with the empty truck but the motor had been ruined by the flood waters and it seized up. Observers could only shake their heads and mutter, "What a waste of taxpayers' money!"

But this family's ordeal wasn't over. Two months after the raid, 24-year old son Clayton loaded his truck with less than $1000 worth of barley he had grown. He headed for the border and was charged there and jailed for seven days. He was finally released after his family paid a $7500 fine and agreed to surrender the truck tractor to Customs.

He would have to pay a $34,400 fine for the old farm truck's return, so he left it with Customs.

W0RSE THAN SELLING MARIJUANA?

Wrote amazed Edmonton Journal columnist Lorne Gunter, "If he had sold marijuana worth the same amount to another adult, its likely, as a first time offender he would have received a conditional discharge. No incarceration. No fine."

Grower Alex McWilliams put this event into a sharper focus. "The Desrochers have farmed for 12 years or more without a wheat board permit, and will never want one ever again. They grow non-board crops they can sell themselves, like canola, flax and sunflowers and barley. They market the oilseeds in fall and winter. They sell the barley in spring and summer to Hutterite colonies who always need feed grain, pay well above wheat board prices, and pay straight weight, no dockage.

"The cash returns compare well with board prices. Their trucks provide side-line revenue and enable them to deliver their crops to the point of best returns.

"Yes," said McWilliams, "more and more farmers are bypassing wheat board crops and have no need for a board permit book."

One thing was becoming clear. The monopoly's vendetta against growers was turning into a publicity nightmare for Ottawa's Liberal government. The media was focusing as never before on this drama of growers braving jail in their survival struggle, making it more difficult for politicians and bureaucrats to depict them as criminal types.

Beyond that, a remarkable revolution was beginning to transform prairie farms, and the entire prairies. Growers like the Desrochers were turning away from monopoly board crops wheat and barley to crops they could sell without government interference. Acreages of canola and mustard and lentils and chickpeas and others were soaring as growers found they could market them effectively themselves and boost their incomes. And all without an abusive marketing nanny.

WHY ARE LAW-ABIDING CITIZENS BREAKING RULES AT GREAT RISK, COST?

Editor/publisher Morris Dorosh has built his newsletter, Agriweek, into a sort of bible for leading growers and grain and agricultural industry people. And as this drama of border crossings and court appearances and trials and jailings of these 'lawbreakers' unfolded, he brought a well-informed mind to comment on it.

He focused on perhaps the most vital truth of all in one column directed not just to his regular readers but to all Canadians and their politicians. "Grain growers who appear to be model law-abiding citizens in all other respects, have taken to consciously breaking the rules. And they are risking grave consequences, disrupting their lives and endangering their assets...But why?"

His answer? "Because no one at the political level is listening to the ground-swelling demand that the Wheat Board be removed from the backs of producers who do not wish its services."

Decades of experience at the heart of this industry left Dorosh with no doubt – the market place works! If you have a product to sell, offer it where people are free to buy or sell as they wish.

Thanks to these border crossings, he told his readers, "all kinds of interesting questions have been raised and all kinds of legal quirks uncovered." And he asked, "Just what is the Canadian Wheat Board? Is it a corporate body 'only' or is it a government regulatory agency? Can or cannot it be both at the same time?

"Can it be alternately a government-owned commercial corporation and a regulator as circumstances suit it? Can a customs duty be levied on goods being exported from the country in the same way as on those being imported? Why are alleged infractions of the Board's export authority not being dealt with under its own legislation (The Canadian Wheat Board Act)?"

And finally Dorosh asked, "If the French and English versions of the same federal regulations do not coincide, which takes precedence and who decides?...Has this Board for 45 years exerted lead-pipe control over the marketing of barley illegally, because no one bothered to renew and confirm its authority as Parliament intended?"

MONOPOLY MARKETING COST GELLERT $125,000 ON ONE CROP

Al Gellert was another grower whose bottom line would have soared if he could have sold directly into that U.S. market in the '95-'96 crop year. He grew about 20,000 bu. of hard red and prairie spring wheat and 40,000 bu. of durum on his 2100-acre Congress, Sask., farm in 1996. And he was continuing to resist the lure of high U.S. wheat prices and to accept woeful cheques from the Ottawa monopoly. The May CWB '95-'96 estimated pool return, with freight and handling deducted, would be about $5.78 a bu. for no. 1 hard red spring wheat, and $6.73 a bu. for durum. Gellert would get $385,000 for his crop.

But just 85 miles away at Scobey, Montana, the spot price with freight and handling deducted, was $C8.75 a bu. for wheat and C$9.10 for durum. Take off 50c a bu. to truck it there and Gellert would still get a cheque for $510,000.

Gellert wanted desperately to believe in the law and to obey it. But the monopoly board wouldn't allow him to deliver his grain there without a buy-back. And it would load on so many costs it would steal his profit. He faced a simple choice. If he obeyed the monopoly, and delivered his grain to it, his one-year loss would be $125,000.

One grower observed wryly, "Of course, the wheat board legislation states the monopoly is responsible for getting what is 'reasonable,' not the best price."

ARE FARMERS ASSHOLES?

But feelings were running high and the pressure finally got to at least one politician whose beliefs were affronted by these brash growers' demands for freedom. CFFJ informed its members in August 1996, of that curious and revealing incident. It reported that an over-heated Saskatchewan NDP cabinet minister named Bernie Wiens had made an unflattering remark about growers who were asking for changes in Wheat Board rules so they could sell their own crops. In fact, he had called them "assholes."

Wiens explained later that he was critical of the way this farm group compared itself with oppressed groups throughout the world.

An outraged CFFJ supporter responded with powerful sarcasm in a letter-to-the-editor. "Mr. Wiens must pine for those halcyon days of Stalinist Russia when a simple bullet in the back of the head was sufficient to deal with political dissenters," she wrote.

WHY DENY GROWERS THE FREEDOM THEY VOTE FOR?

Earlier in that fateful year of '96, CFFJ presented further devastating evidence showing why more and more growers were joining in these crossings. A news release signed by members Ken Severson, Dale Paterson, Darroll Wallin and Gerald Blerot on Feb. 28 reported barley was worth $2.80 per bu. in Kamsack, Sask. But it was worth nearly twice that – C$5.45 – in Berthold, N.D.

Severson added irony or perhaps whimsy, in a later (July 5) news release – "In Russia people elected Boris Yeltsin for democracy and free choice. In Canada we have…a dictatorship, and no choice...Wheat and barley growers have no options on where to market their grain. It's the CWB or nothing."

And he offered telling evidence that grower support for the monopoly was slumping – a recent Alberta vote where "...65% of farmers favoured dual marketing (in which growers would be free to sell their own grain.)" A Saskatchewan government survey found, "...58% of farmers supported dual marketing."

Wheat board Chief Lorne Hehn tried to counter that attack, reporting in the spring, '96, edition of AgWorld, a study which seemed to be based on confidential board information. It claimed to show the monopoly got premiums of $13.35 per tonne on western red spring milling wheat sales over a 14-year period. Economists/researchers Kraft, Furtan and Tyrchniewicz who did the study, said these benefits might increase to $30 per tonne. But they wouldn't exist at all if some growers were free to sell their own grain.

Grower Jim Pallister rejected that study based on such secret information. And he held up a newer one by researchers Dr. Al Loyns and Dr. Colin Carter which he said was based on the experiences of a range of farmers. It showed conclusively, he said, "The wheat board doesn't put more dollars in my pocket."

Pallister added, "Anyone needing an economic explanation as to why more and more farmers want the Chretien Wheat Board's monopoly to end now has it with the release of the Carter/Loyns study."

HIGHWAY SIGNS SCREAM OUT MESSAGE – GROWERS JAILED FOR SELLING GRAIN

The news media were soon reporting (Sept, 96,) another startling CFFJ initiative which put further pressure on Wheat Board Minister Goodale and the left wing political elite who were denying growers their freedom. These growers painted a huge 8 ft. by 12 ft. sign and set it up on the U.S.-Canada border at Regway, 2 hours drive south of Regina,to greet U.S. visitors to Canada. It screamed out its blazing message:

> "WELCOME TO CANADA...THE ONLY FREE COUNTRY IN THE WORLD THAT IMPRISONS FARMERS FOR SELLING THEIR OWN GRAIN.

That sign dramatised the plight of the imprisoned Andy McMechan, aiming to help swing public opinion behind him and other freedom-seeking growers. More farmers were soon joined in this escapade, displaying similar signs from their own farms to highway travellers. The news media sent out cameramen and reporters to record these messages and to inform their audiences across the country.

Growers displaying such signs soon got warning letters from the Highways Department which controls such signage, ordering them, "Get those signs down."

But the free-market growers refused to blink. Leader Art Mainil of Benson, Sask., answered if it came down to a crunch, growers would mount the signs on the sides of trucks. Or move them from farm to farm. He said similar signs were already planned for the border crossing points of

Portal, Oungre, and Cornonach.

One sign was even destined for Solicitor-General Herb Gray's riding in Windsor, Ont., where it would greet tens of thousands of U.S. visitors at that heavy-traffic point. And support for this Windsor initiative was widespread. Grower Russ Larson broke the good news that the plea to growers and others for donations of $1300 to erect that sign was greatly oversubscribed. One cheque even came from an Ontario farm group leader.

A sign mounted on a flatbed truck that could be easily moved back and forth among farms as the warnings came out, remained for over two years along Hwy. 1 near Regina. The government finally gave up the battle, yielded to the growers' will.

MORE CROSSINGS TO BRING BACK PROCESSING, OPPORTUNITY TO WEST

To keep up the pressure, CFFJ growers called another crossing for Portal for April 10, proclaiming their motto was, "To obtain Dual Marketing for western farmers by defending our legal rights." And they focused on the most devastating cost of this monopoly and the central reason for their freedom crusade – "The wheat board has destroyed processing and opportunity in Western Canada."

It challenged growers, "Let's haul grain. Join in moving bagged grain or flour in your pickup or car. And return to Canada Customs at Portal before noon April 11. Your wheat is worth over $8 per bu. in Plentywood, Berthold, and Bottineau, and buyers want it. Now is the time to break this contemptible illusion of a monopoly and all the injustice it represents."

It promised the upcoming crossing would be "...the biggest wave yet of farmers...defying Ottawa's destructive Control of Western Grain. Farmers will assemble at the Husky station in Estevan."

MORE GOOD NEWS!

CFFJ now reported almost triumphantly that growers prairie-wide were joining in this freedom struggle, and support pledges had reached $9500. The Prairie Farm Commodity Coalition, which represented growers of almost every grain, oilseed and special crop grown in the west, was in full agreement with them. And these two groups wanted the monopoly cut back to a corporation brokering overseas grain sales, mainly government-to-government, to countries such as China and Japan.

Peace River, Alta., grower Bill Blake now stated publicly, "The Wheat Board is coming apart. It is a relic from a bygone time, and has no role in a modern liberalised global trading era." He predicted, "Dual marketing is imminent."

But these growers still faced a mountainous challenge. Perhaps 150 farmers in towns like Lyleton, Brandon, Lethbridge and Estevan, had charges pending connected with by-passing the monopoly and selling grain illegally. And CFFJ called another crossing for May 1, reminding growers, "The Desrochers family and Duane Forrester were brutalised." It urged them, "To help these farmers financially, call Duane or Norm or bring a cheque to Portal on Wednesday."

The trucks would be "...leaving early and back to Portal during the afternoon. Join us for lunch at the OUTBACK in Portal May 1st. If you can't haul grain, please come to support a free market for free people. We'll show these people what courage and determination is out there."

5

GROWERS VOTE FOR FREEDOM; MONOPOLY TARGETS COMMUNITY LEADERS IN 'DEATH-WISH' REFUSAL TO SELL BARLEY

In trying desperately to enforce its monopoly, Ottawa was targeting dozens of growers who were also community and spiritual leaders. Intimidation was its tool. And freedom-loving farmers with remarkable stories to tell were moving into this struggle. Some families had even fled communism.

GROWERS TRUE TO THEIR ALBERTA HERITAGE

More than the people in any other province, Albertans believe in the genius of the people, not the politicians. They cherish personal freedom and responsibility - a formula that has been the key to their soaring prosperity and surging population growth despite the monopoly board's intrusive impact.

Yes, perhaps the most dynamic economy in Canada. Young people from Saskatchewan and Manitoba and from British Columbia too were streaming into the province to get jobs and to invest to create wealth. Businessmen were transferring head offices there to seize the benefit of low taxes and the dynamic economy and an atmosphere where new ideas could be openly discussed and even embraced. A parade of retiring seniors were moving there to escape high taxes in other provinces. So in this controversy-plagued grain-marketing issue, nobody could doubt that Alberta's political and business leaders solidly supported the free market.

But in late 1995, with protests against the monopoly board escalating across the prairies, Alberta's Agriculture Minister Walter Paszkowski wanted to be certain of growers' views on this freedom issue. He called a historic vote and announced the unsurprising results on Dec. 6.

By almost 2 to 1, growers had pleaded for change. They voted for freedom to opt out of the Wheat Board monopoly and to sell their own wheat and barley. Of 16,151 farmers who had registered, 10,452 favoured the dual market for barley, 9,701 favoured it for wheat. They wanted to keep government cut down to size and politicians and bureaucrats out of people's personal and business affairs.

The only question was, "Would Ottawa listen?"

ANOTHER CROSSING EXPLODES INTO A FIRESTORM – 18 CHARGED

Many of those growers had joined Farmers for Justice to help lead the freedom struggle. One of them was Rick Strankman of Altario.

By any standard, the Strankmans are community leaders. Most people would consider this family a role model. Wife Dianne is a retired Wardair Flight attendant. Rick and Dianne have a son Jay, and daughter Pamela, who were then aged 6 and 4. Rick himself worked for ten years as a school bus driver. He is a former Queen's Scout, served as Chairman of the School Council, is a former member for Chinook Applied Research, and was a Board member for Dry Country Gas Co-op. He is also a Flying Farmer, a member of the Canadian Aerial Applicators and an Alberta Aerial Applicator.

Rick was at the centre of a border crossing at Coutts, AB., in late April, '96, that exploded into a firestorm. Calgary Herald reporter Donald Campbell was on the spot and he wrote, "Farmers fighting (Ottawa's) control of their grain will now have to fight to regain control of their grain trucks after getting nabbed for illegally exporting to the US Tuesday."

He went on, "Eighteen farmers were charged with violating Canada Customs legislation by trucking grain Monday to Montana...Farmers driving seven large grain trucks, 10 pick-up trucks and a car were stopped and charged upon their return to Alberta at noon Tuesday. They were also informed that their trucks have been seized by Canada Customs and bright red stickers were pasted to the windows...(warning): 'These goods are under customs seizure, do not remove.'

"But the farmers who held a strategy session Monday night in Shelby, Montana, refused to turn over the keys to their vehicles. They drove the convoy from the Canada Customs compound in a horn-blaring highway grain train, while customs agents videotaped them."

An Acadia Valley farmer who had sold 800 Bu. in Montario for 25 percent more than he would get from the wheat board, told Campbell, "I intend to ignore this seizure and drive out of here today to make my point that I want to freely market my grain."

Campbell reported, "Western Barley Growers' Association President Buck Spencer called Tuesday's harvest by the federal government 'a terrible, absolutely terrible event. The only criminals here are the federal government.'"

When Rick Strankman wrote his own report hours later to inform CFFJ members and the media of these happenings, he called it, "..a very successful convoy. Growers were finding out what their grain was really worth – not the Wheat Board price. And at these US elevators, virtually all grades priced at over $8 Can."

Weeks earlier Strankman had put this issue into a broader perspective in a CFFJ news release he entitled, "Your Money or Your Life." He wrote, "All western farmers are poorer because of the Chretien Wheat Board's control."

And he focused on one simple but outrageous fact. "McMechan is supposed to pay $55,000 for export licences while eastern farmers get export permits free. How could that be justified?" he asked.

Strankman was now putting every ounce of his energy into winning freedom for growers to manage their own farms. But meanwhile, FFJ reported that Ottawa's monopoly board would be asking to have him incarcerated for the maximum six months sentence.

MASS ARRESTS AT COUTTS – COMMUNITY, SPIRITUAL LEADERS IN COURT

That Coutts crossing again put this freedom/survival issue into a clear and cruel perspective. Those higher US prices might still save their farms from bankruptcy and enable them to continue building their communities and their churches, and educating their kids. But those eighteen growers who were charged were summoned to appear in Lethbridge court to face 'justice.'

Here surely was an astonishing twist in Canada's story – an issue that went deep into Canada's very soul. What madness had descended on the country when these and dozens of other community and church leaders and normally law-abiding citizens were being arrested and many of them pitched into jail for selling grain they grew themselves, to waiting US buyers? Yet mounting evidence was convincing these growers they had broken no law.

And if they had, they asked, "Why do we have a law that denies us the right to earn a living?" No wonder they were now telling their stories through the media of how those market prices were the key to their survival.

A surprising list of growers were charged and haled into court. Russell Barrows had begun farming in 1951 after attending the Olds School of Agriculture in Alberta. He and his wife Rose raised four children on their 2500-acre grain and livestock farm at Coutts. Now they enjoyed nine grandchildren.

Russell is a strong community leader. He has been director of the recreation board at Coutts and Chairman of the Coutts Agricultural Society. And he served on both the Volunteer Committee and the Cemetery Committee there. He designed a three-green golf and driving range under irrigation. He has also been a church pastor, and he has administered a Christian school. He has done missionary work in India, Haiti and Southern Mexico and he has had three separate assignments to Africa.

Son Wayne is a chip off the old block. He began farming in 1983 and Russell still helps him. He also was serving on the Board of Directors of the Fantasta Pasta plant. And he was a member of the Agricultural Society.

Yes, Russell Barrows is respected by numberless Albertans for his community work and leadership and by people around the world for his missionary work. But he had to go to court.

"OUR RIGHTS HAVE BEEN TAKEN FROM US"

Robert C Thomas farms at Warner, AB, and he was also charged in that crossing. Like so many farmers, he has always known how to work hard and get things done so he could find time to offer leadership in his community. Thomas has been President of the Agricultural Mechanics Department at the Southern Alberta Institute of Technology. He has been a school bus driver and president of the curling club. For three years he was area rep for Alberta Wheat Pool. He has been coach for women's slow pitch, and an officer of the Elk's Club.

He has also been a Minor Hockey coach, a basketball coach, a church board member, a Scout troop helper, a director of a gas co-op, and a member of the Parents Advisory Committee at Warner school. He was Board member of the Safflower Growers Assoc., and he worked part time with Agricultural Financial Services. He also worked with his son on the farm.

Thomas' wife is a registered nurse. Their three children are well-educated young adults. Yes, this family has always been at the very heart of their community.

But Thomas had serious concerns. "I have spent most of my life farming with the hope of creating a future for my children and their children. A family farm is a wonderful place to raise a family. And changes must be made...to keep our future generations here.

"I always felt Canada was a democratic country, but...our right to make choices has been taken from us. We pay to own the land, we pay the taxes and the input costs, we pay machinery costs to farm the land. But as for the fruits of our labour, we have no control in the market place. And we continue to pay."

He found the lesson of that Coutts crossing was unmistakable. "Wheat Board changes must come. We need a dual marketing system giving us the freedom to decide where and how to market our products."

Farmers for Justice leaders asked, "Why does Ottawa consider Robert C Thomas a criminal?"

JAIL THOSE FARMERS! IT'S THE CANADIAN WAY

Another couple who got caught in this nightmare were Jim and Sharon Ness who were raising their children Jon, 16, and Amber, 18, on their farm at New Brigden, AB. These family members had all been busy in activities at the very heart of their community. Jim was director of the 1200-member Dry Country Gas Co-op., and of the Cereal Christian

Centre. He was manager of the Hannah Girls' Hockey team in 1995. You would be hard-pressed to find a selfish bone in any of the members of this hard working family.

Yes, every community wants people like these. Yet it seemed the monopoly board aimed to have Jim imprisoned for a maximum 6-months sentence because he wanted to sell his own grain, reported CFFJ.

Doyle Winczura and his wife Joyce have been at the very centre of an endless round of community activities in their Viking, AB, home community. They donated time and equipment to the Viking golf course when it was built. Doyle also plays recreational hockey with the local hockey team.

But when he sold his own wheat, Ottawa's single desk seller said he must pay. He was hauled off to criminal court. Yet wife Joyce doesn't think he's a criminal. Nor do his children Michelle, Cheryl and Devon think he should go to jail. Nor do his hockey team-mates think he belongs behind bars.

Two other victims were **Darren and Jane Winczura** who with their kids Ashley and Blake, also farm at Viking, Alta. This family too is at the very centre of their community. Darren attended Red Deer College and got his Journeyman in water well drilling. He began farming in 1988 after the untimely death of his father in a plane crash. Their family life is filled with hockey. Darren played in the Saskatchewan Jr. Hockey League from '85 to '88, and he coached the Nipawin All Star team in '88. He coached the Midgets in Viking to the provincials from 1992 to 94. And he taught power skating to elementary and jr.-high aged skaters from '88 to '90.

But farming is a serious business for Darren, and he knows that marketing is crucial to success. So he sold his own grain for the highest price he could get. And Ottawa charged him.

H. Noel Hyslip who farms at Vulcan, AB, along with wife Deb and their kids Megan, Jay, and Erin, was also trapped in this conflict. Noel has always been immersed in community activities. But he sold his own grain so he had to be charged. It seems to be the Canadian way. This story of crime and criminal charges goes on and on.

LESS TIME FOR FARMING AND FAMILY ACTIVITIES

Saskatchewan growers had also joined that Coutts crossing and Gregory Ross McIntyre was among them. Greg and his wife Tammy and their kids Ryan and Kelly, then aged 9 and 6, farm at D'Arcy, Sask. Like more and more farmers today, Greg understands perfectly - marketing is just as vital to success on a farm as is production.

That's why he grows a range of crops including durum, lentils, mustard and peas. It's all part of today's revolution in farming. And Greg enjoys marketing his own crops. He has sold his own board grain to get needed revenue. And like hundreds of other growers, he has been hauled into court for doing it.

Not surprisingly, this busy family resents the criminal charges laid against him in that Lethbridge courthouse. Greg is a busy community worker. He's a past president of the local crop club, a board member of the local United Grain Growers and a trustee of the local school board. Tammy is busy too as a skiing teacher and as a spare bus driver.

Family members say it's just the monopoly that thinks he **is a criminal**. And these charges mean he must defend himself, leaving him less time for his myriad community commitments and less time for the family to work together on the farm and to have fun together.

IN VENDETTA AGAINST GROWERS, DOES ART WALDE DESERVE JAIL OR A HALO?

Ottawa's vendetta against this widening range of leading farmers continued unabated. In a Nov. 27 news release, FFJ reported, "**..14 farmers were in court in Lethbridge,**" and it named some of these 'criminals.' **One of them was Art Walde** who with his wife Sylvia, farmed at Kindersley, Sask.

The Waldes have four married children and 11 grandchildren. They are forever busy in church and community activities and with farm groups. Art was active in the Reform party and the politics that play such an overwhelming role in shaping the prairies. He has been a member of the Odd Fellows Lodge; was on the Save Our Soils committee, and in the crop club and other farm groups. And he worked on behalf of seniors and young people and of the school board and other good causes. His one crime was he wanted to market his own grain and he got caught up in this issue which haunts the prairies. So Farmers for Justice said he was in the sights of the monopoly board.

Art was in court along with eleven other farmers in

Nov. '97. His crime? He took 50 pounds of barley across the US border, defying the CWB's export monopoly. He donated that grain to Rev. Keith Dangerfield, who was in charge of the 4-H Club in Sunburst, Montana.

If convicted, Art faced a heavy fine, possibly imprisonment. In court, he sat on an iron-hard oak bench as the crown prosecutor urged the judge to deal harshly with him so as to discourage other farmers from "criminal" acts. But was this really a criminal act? What had motivated Art?

WOMEN RAPED, PROPERTY DESTROYED, WALDE'S FAMILY FLED COMMUNISM

Art's family story puts this into a devastating perspective. His grandparents were among those who left Germany when Catherine the Great sought industrious people to populate the fertile southern steppes. That was before World War 1. These people lived in the small village of Orloff. And as the war was ending, the retreating German army saw these former Germans as a source of desperately needed food and supplies. They traded firearms for food.

But the Communists were then emerging. Russians were fighting among themselves. And marauding bands of thieves posing as revolutionaries were common. These thieves knew the people of Orloff had guns and left them alone.

When the revolution ended and the new regime took control, the people turned over their weapons to the government. And they paid a desperate price. A marauding band which had aligned itself with the Communists then sacked Orloff. Women were raped, property destroyed or stolen. Art Walde's grandfather was one of forty-four men brutally killed. The lower part of his face and part of his left cheek were blown away.

Art's dad Abram and Art's mom were born in the southern Ukraine and survived this massacre. Abram with his young wife and a baby daughter (Art's older sister) were among the very last to get out legally in the 1920's. They travelled by boxcar and as the train moved north, the communist police were patrolling. Often a man or woman would be taken off the train for 'questioning' never to be seen again.

When the train crossed into Latvia and to freedom, the small group scrambled out onto the ground, dropped to their knees and tearfully sang a hymn of thanks to Almighty God.

They had survived the tyranny.

Abram Walde moved on to Kindersley, Sask., where Art was born a few years later.

Yes, Art knows from this story of his ancestors, what tyranny and lack of freedom and justice are about. And after he left court in 1997, he put the matter into a crystal clear perspective. "The real issue isn't grain or even money," he said. "Its individual freedom. People find it difficult to realise why we must move to freedom."

Who can better judge that real issue than Art Walde?

BARLEY FIASCO MAY HAVE COST $180 MILLION; BESWICK QUIT $100,000 JOB

Ken Beswick is a soft-spoken Albertan who has made a huge success of his own grain farm. He has also won the respect of neighbouring growers and many others across the west who know him. As a young idealist with a sense of public service, he accepted an appointment as a Wheat Board Commissioner. It was his way of helping to improve the system to benefit all growers. But he too became alarmed at the devastating damage being imposed on the West and on Canada itself by Ottawa's monopoly.

Beswick's concern came to a head in the 1994-95 year. More and more barley growers were becoming convinced the board's pool price wasn't working. The pooling was too rigid and inflexible, and the bureaucratic system enforcing it couldn't transmit timely market signals. The result was inevitable. Barley sometimes flowed into export markets when it was worth more at home. And sometimes the opposite occurred.

Beswick said such a fiasco in the '94-'95 crop year may have cost growers $180 million - more than the whole feed barley pool was worth. He said 9 million tonnes of barley were used in the domestic market, but it sold for $20 a tonne less than it would have fetched in the competitive global market - a $180 million loss. And it might have been more. Yes, low prices resulted from incompetent marketing. And they cost growers a fortune.

With the system failing, Beswick saw only one solution. The wheat board must change its ways, end price pooling for feed barley, replace it with buying barley on a daily cash price basis or world price. When nothing happened, he resigned from the Board.

FFJ member Richard Nordstrom issued a news release on May 1, '96, to focus public attention on Beswick's brave act. He wrote, "It is inspiring to see an individual do the honourable thing and stand on principal. Mr. Beswick knew farmers were not being treated right and their interests not being served by the monopoly. He must have found the situation intolerable."

The Viking, Alta., grower added that Beswick had left a job paying well over $100,000 a year. And Nordstrom said Beswick's involvement was the **last hope of a part of Western agriculture** that felt the Wheat Board could be changed from inside.

"Now that hope dies," he said. "Dual marketers are not represented at the commissioner level or on the advisory committee. So the total intransigence there is sure to deepen."

What might happen next? Nordstrom saw no easy way out, predicted, "All the forces of reform will now focus relentlessly on changing the legislation to end the monopoly and forget about trying to work with the Wheat Board."

"DEATH WISH" REFUSAL TO EXPORT BARLEY PROVES INCOMPETENCE - SPENCER

With the struggle intensifying in early '96, Alberta growers formed a "Marketing Choice Implementation Group" to help those who wanted to win their freedom. And hard-nosed Western Barley Growers President Buck Spencer wrote a news release revealing the seething unrest.

"Farmer frustration boils ...as the CWB rejects 50% of ...feed barley contract," he wrote. "The CWB refusal to export feed barley offered by grain farmers when world stocks are at record lows proves incompetence...denies farmers access to $4.15 per Bu., causing a 25% loss."

The wheat board's "..death wish is brought closer by the incredible lack of sensitivity this single desk monopoly has for its grain farmer slaves," he added, predicting civil disobedience was "..virtually guaranteed to continue," because it resulted from the CWB's "inability to understand the tools needed by modern innovative farmers."

What are those tools? "Access to reliable risk management tools available in the International market place is the foundation on which many of these grain farmers seek to build a stable and profitable...business," he stated. "Last week's pathetic display by the National Farmers' Union, SaskPool, the CWB and Manitoba Pool insisting that canola be put under a single desk monopoly and be pooled, was a new height of arrogance," he added.

In Spencer's view, this debate revealed again the hopelessness of finding a reasonable solution to the marketing needs of modern grain agriculture. "The raping of the integrity of the feed barley pooling account is dramatic proof - the CWB has no credibility and its management system is incapable of managing grain farmers' marketing needs."

No, the wheat board lacked accountability to farmers. Growers had no appeal panel where they could question its arbitrary decisions.

HUNGER-STRIKING GROWER ASKS PROBE INTO BOARD

Secretary of that new Marketing Choice Group was Thomas R Jackson who had come into conflict with the board when it denied him the freedom to market his pedigreed seed wheat without a license. He challenged its jurisdiction and lost. But he was an unlikely target for Ottawa's monopoly and for the Liberal government directing it.

Jackson and his family farm over 7000 acres of land at Ardrossan, AB., growing seed and commercial crops including wheat, barley, canola, peas and forage for seed and hay. He is the fourth generation of his family there, a pillar of his church, and a man of deep religious faith. He places just about every act, whether personal or business, in moral terms. He aims to be right with his God.

But in the mid-'90's, it happened. Prairie growers were increasingly restless with those regulations denying them the freedom to manage their own farms, and to sell their home-grown wheat and barley. And now Tom was charged with ignoring those rules. Yes, he had trucked his pedigreed seed wheat to the US where eager buyers paid much more than he could get from Ottawa's monopoly. But now he faced Ottawa's wrath. He was hauled into court in 1996.

Tom Jackson is short in stature but impressively broad, even beefy. He once went on a hunger strike to back his position. His endless energy means he doesn't go unnoticed at meetings and in crowds. And his powerful faith gives him an unusual strength. He doesn't intimidate easily. He can be zealous in defending his principles. He was convinced he had broken no law, but rather had acted in Canada's best interests and in his own as well.

He believes implicitly in straight talk, and he sent Wheat Board Minister Goodale a probing letter in March, '96, (with copies to Prime Minister Chretien, Agriculture Minister Vanclief, Opposition MP's and Alberta Agriculture Minister Paszkowski,) requesting "..an official in-camera judicial hearing...into the horrendous activities of the CWB in ...handling prairie barley."

He also asked pointedly if the Board's Western Barley Contract compromised the Winnipeg Commodity Exchange's integrity. And he accused the CWB of "..intentionally mishandling its authority re the financial returns of domestic Western Canadian feed barley producers...by ... restricting exports of feed barley."

STUDY THE LEGAL ISSUES

In preparing for his 1996 court trial, Jackson had set out to educate himself on the legal issues. He researched Parliament's intentions in setting it up and the legislation enforcing it. He dug into the politics which had transformed the priceless prairie grain industry into one where politics reigned supreme (growers quip, only half-jokingly, that wheat is 15% protein and 85% politics,) and business is little more than an afterthought.

Yes, he was to the very heart of Western Canada's long-running struggle to finally free itself from Ottawa's tyranny which prevents it from fully developing its resources treasure house and becoming a full partner in Confederation.

Jackson lost his 1996 court case. But it never occurred to him to simply submit to Ottawa's will. He regarded his conviction as unthinking and unjust treatment from Big Brother. And he proceeded on to the federal Court of Appeal in '97. When it denied his defense in early 2000, he again saw the struggle as just beginning.

He wrote a ringing response to the court. And with a symbolism that could not have cried out more loudly, he chose July 1, Dominion Day, to present it to the Judicial Council, the Chief Justice of the federal Court of Canada and to the citizens of Canada.

EVIDENCE SHOWED BOARD BREACHED LAW

Jackson laid out his case. His research had convinced him the Wheat Board was breaching the British North America Act, the Canadian Bill of Rights, the Canadian Wheat Board Act, the Canada Grain Act and the Criminal Code of Canada, as well as what he called "the Great Commandment" and sections of Deuteronomy in the Bible. No, he was not simply arguing law. This was a matter of right or wrong. He had no doubt he was on the side of right, and he and increasing numbers of growers must eventually prevail.

His evidence showed that the monopoly lacked the power to refuse growers export licenses and to impose Buy-Back procedures on them because those actions are not in the interests of grain growers. Parliament's goal in passing the legislation was to serve growers' interests. And because of the Canadian Bill of Rights and the provinces' control over property and civil rights, he said grain cannot be confiscated, "..without respect for the owner's enjoyment of his/her personal property."

If the wheat board had to respond to market forces, and to respect the best interests of all growers, he said grain prices would rise to all growers "..until equilibrium was reached." Then if the board's prices and services equaled or bettered those for grain marketed outside the monopoly, this would respect each grower's rights and serve the best interests of all.

CANADIANS HAVE FEWER PROPERTY RIGHTS

He turned to another issue that was catching growers' attention - that Canadians have fewer property rights than people of other countries under the North American Free Trade Act (NAFTA.) Yet Canada has signed the United Nations Declaration which says everyone is entitled to all the rights and freedoms set forth for race, color, sex, language, religion, political or other opinion, and more. If the Canadian Bill of Rights was applied as intended, he said, "..through the intent of God's law, which is the foundation for the Rule of Law," then Canadians could not have fewer property rights.

Jackson also said he had notified the monopoly's corporate secretary and the Justice Solicitor in Dec., 1999, that these neglected issues needed to be dealt with. But the only response was that the CWB would see him in court and the Court would look after his concerns. He ignored this snub and urged the Court to allow growers to freely use their own wheat (and thus to sell it for the highest possible price) if it has not been graded under the Canada Grain Act. For the Law doesn't force a grower to get his grain so graded.

MINISTER'S ARROGANT RESPONSE TO PANEL'S DEFIANCE

This had now become more than a struggle to reshape the massive prairie grain industry. These growers were examining the West's role in Canada and the shape of Canada itself. And more and more grain industry players were being caught up in its politics.

Minister Goodale had created a Western Grain Marketing Panel to recommend needed changes in the system. And he was undoubtedly confident his Panel members would recognise what he called an unquestioned truth - growers were unable to market their own wheat and barley effectively - the government board must remain all-powerful. These members included prominent growers Bill Duke, Jack Gorr and Owen McAuley who clearly wanted change. But Farmers For Justice grower Curtis Sims of MacGregor, Man., looked at the additional non-grower Panel members, and asked in a news release, "Over 90% of the money invested in this industry is on the farms. So why is our future in the hands of elevator interests, an eastern miller, a pensioned Wheat Board commissioner and a Liberal lawyer?"

Sims added, "This is an extension of Goodale's arrogant and condescending attitude towards rural people."

Yet when that panel reported in July, '96, it called for big changes in the board and big marketing reforms. Those words must have hit the minister as a massive heresy. Yes, the panel said the board should continue to market most classes of wheat. But it reversed direction 180 degrees for feed barley and organic grains such as specialty wheat.

"Sell these grains on the open market," it urged. It also asked Goodale to allow each farmer to sell up to 25% of his crop outside the board.

Here was a direct challenge to the minister's power and to Liberal dogma. A shocked Goodale would have none of it. In a 'letter to the editor,' he betrayed his lack of faith in prairie growers and perhaps even in the democratic process, declaring, "The fractious nature of the grain industry...makes it impossible for farmers themselves to reach a consensus."

He continued with awesome arrogance, **"...the government must assume the responsibility of running a multibillion dollar industry that has become the backbone of the prairies."**

That response served to bond these free market growers, setting up three high-profile antagonists – the Board, the Minister, and the Liberal government. And by midsummer of '96, over 100 farmers who supported this panel's cry for marketing reforms and especially to free up feed barley and specialty wheat, had made the border run and were charged.

MONOPOLY "A JOLLY ROGER TITANIC, HEADING FOR AN ICEBERG."

Now Tom Jackson threw himself further into this quickening struggle, attending gatherings and meetings across the prairies. His challenge was to help create an image of this festering issue in human terms that the public could understand. Then they could demand corrective political action.

He began referring to the monopoly as a Pirate ship, and as the Jolly Roger Titanic that was heading for an iceberg.

He wired the Prime Minister, "We will never surrender. All it takes for Evil to prevail is for good people to do nothing." He urged all growers, "Call your MP. Call your MLA."

In one initiative, he put his fertile imagination to work and dreamed up a curious hypothesis that Ottawa had attacked auto makers the way it did farmers. Then, tongue firmly in cheek, he related how Ottawa had set up a monopoly board to sell all Ford and Chevy vehicles. This board was pooling these vehicle sales for the year, then returning the average selling price to the car makers.

He dubbed it the Canadian Vehicle Board, or CVB. And he said that under this wheat-board-like monopoly if a Ford producer wanted to sell a new vehicle into the US, he must first sell it to the CVB. Then he could buy it back at a much higher price just like prairie grain growers do with their wheat.

Jackson hypothesized further that many car makers were complaining that CVB exports to Asia Pacific countries and South America were being made at bargain basement prices. This lowered the pool values. And the car makers protested that American auto makers were getting 25% more for their vehicles and parts on average, than their Canadian cousins, without including subsidies.

To drive home his parallel with wheat growers, Jackson claimed that some of those vehicle manufacturers had placed a sign at the Windsor-Detroit bridge crying out...

"CANADA, THE ONLY COUNTRY IN THE FREE WORLD THAT THROWS ITS VEHICLE MANUFACTURERS IN JAIL FOR SELLING THEIR OWN VEHICLES."

He fantasized that smaller manufacturers were now telling the large ones they must continue to cross-subsidize them. And many of them, both large and small, were complaining that the monopoly was bankrupting them by selling Cadillac cars at Lada prices.

Strangely, said Jackson, some smaller manufacturers had joined in the protest, saying the CVB's actions were wrong and must stop.

No, that fictional story didn't really happen to car makers. The public would never allow it. But it was happening every day to prairie grain farmers, so why didn't the public cry out?

WHEAT BOARD LACKS LEGAL CONTROL

Jackson challenged the court to find Parliament's intent when it extended its authority into the grain handling system. The Wheat Board Act was recreated in 1947 and the Canada Grain Act had been examined critically in the courts He had asked Ottawa in 1998 to analyse the Wheat Board Act's impact regarding the Charter of Rights and Freedoms and the Canadian Bill of Rights. But to his knowledge these studies were never done, so he assumed their original intent was still valid.

He found that Alberta hadn't authorized the CWB to encroach on its jurisdiction over grain. And for good reason. Like all provinces, Alberta holds exclusive jurisdiction under the BNA Act. Property and civil rights there must not be breached. The Canada Grain Act was shaped over the years to avoid these Constitutional questions.

In fact, he found the Wheat Board Act only regulates grain after it leaves the growers' control and is graded under the Canada Grain Act. But growers have the right to decide if and when this will happen. This avoided conflicts with the provinces which hold exclusive jurisdiction under the BNA Act. Yes, growers can gain the protection of the Canada Grain Act by getting their produce graded under it. And if they don't, they will be totally responsible for all aspects of selling it, without any protection from Ottawa through it.

WHAT ABOUT JACKSON'S SEED GRAIN?

Focusing on his own case, Jackson said "seed grain" is not a Canada Grain Act grain. And if Ottawa had intended the CWB to control export of his pedigreed seed wheat, it would have to change both the CWB Act, and the Canada Grain Act. But it can't unless Alberta agrees and passes concurring legislation. And his civil and property rights in Ottawa's jurisdiction would have to be extinguished to do this.

He said that in his original case, Hon. Justice Rothstein ignored the fact that no law requires him to grade his seed grain, or any other raw grain under the Canada Grain Act. He said his own Wildcat wheat is not considered by the CWB to be equal or better than Glenlea, as is required by the Canada Grain Act. So it is a "non Canada Grain Act grain."

Jackson also asked why the CWB export license document has not been gazetted and filed as part of the CWB regulations. For Parliament intended the Export License to pertain to The Trade in grain, but not to grain farmers, as "the Act does not purport to give the Board complete control of all grain grown in those provinces within the designated area to which the Act applies."

Yes, he said an undisputed CWB monopoly existed in 1943 because of the Second World War. But Ottawa ended the War Measures Act in 1947, and the CWB had to give up many of the powers that were not constitutional in peacetime. And now it had no power to force growers to sell to the board if it was not in their best interests.

Jackson said if growers could export more of their own

grain, then Canadian graded grain would become scarcer forcing up the price. Since Canada has plenty of grain to fill all premium markets, he said when he exports his own grain, he is bestowing a benefit upon the other growers in the designated area, by reducing the volume of lower value CWB grain available.

And he said if his own grain has a higher value when sold in the US, that extra value doesn't come from anything the CWB did, but only from things he did.

6

JUDGE RULES AGAINST HISTORIC CHARTER CHALLENGE

Twenty one growers launched the Calgary Charter Challenge on the constitutional validity and the effects of the Wheat Board Act in June, '96. They were supported by the Western Barley Growers Assoc. and the Alberta Barley Commission. Judge Muldoon devastated their hopes.

CROWN BUREAUCRAT FLAUNTS CONTEMPT FOR GROWERS

With those mass arrests triggering increasing outrage among farmers and the farm community, growers went back to the drawing board. Twenty-one of them decided to turn up the pressure another notch, and joined with the high profile Western Barley Growers Association as well as the Alberta government's Barley Commission. Their goal was to launch a historic Charter Challenge to question the constitutional validity and effects of the Canadian Wheat Board Act.

The case went to federal court in Calgary in Oct., '96, and the growers laid out their evidence. Under the Act, it seemed, all grain elevators, railway cars, etc., within the designated area were deemed to be "for the general advantage of Canada" rather than for the advantage of growers themselves and the West. And "flour mills, feed mills, feed warehouses and seed cleaning mills" were also declared to be for the general advantage of Canada.

"But what about the growers' interests?" they asked. Why wasn't the board bound to maximize return to growers?

They told how the Act restricted their freedom to manage their farms and to market their grain to the best advantage. And it prevented them moving aggressively into processing their raw grain to increase its value, creating wealth and jobs.

This Charter Challenge triggered a desperate response by some bureaucrats, revealing a shocking indifference to the human issues involved. One Crown representative asked each farmer the breathtaking question, "Is there anything in the CWB Act that prevents you from moving outside the designated area of the Prairies?"

The Prime Minister himself might well have stepped in following such a comment to assure all Canadians that such remarks by people on the public payroll were unacceptable. But he didn't.

"NO STATE MARKETING WHEN MY GRANDFATHER CAME HERE FLEEING OPPRESSION"

Paul Orsak was in court to hear that scathing question. And he kept his feelings on a tight leash. Orsak and his dad farm 3800 acres near Binscarth, MB, sharing equipment and labor. Paul seeds about 30% canola and 20% peas. Crop rotation needs force him to seed half wheat which he must sell through the monopoly. But the monopoly interferes with his efforts to plan adequate cash flow. And the buy-back robs him of any possible profit from his own sales. To make ends meet, he must sometimes sell off-Board crops at the wrong times when prices are down.

But now Orsak responded carefully to that astounding question from the Crown. "The government seems to be saying the CWB monopoly is an unchanging feature of Western Canada just like the Rockies, cold winters and mosquitoes - one either accepts it or he must move out."

He set out his position in unmistakable terms. "When my grandfather came here fleeing oppression, there was no compulsory state marketing. And I am determined along with thousands of others, to have a freer system right here.

"My wife and I have five children. We have grandparents just a few miles down the road, and we have deep roots in the area. My family and many others would rather stay and fight to change the marketing system.

"The Crown does not seem to grasp how deep our commitment is to our communities and to western Canada," said Orsak. "It would be a tremendous personal and business upheaval to leave (our home and in fact, everything we have built in our lifetime.)

"It is because we are staying that we want this oppressive and inhibiting system changed for our future and for our children."

"OPEN MARKET WILL BOOST RETURNS" - HIGH PROFILE ECONOMIST

Powerful testimony also came from agricultural economist Dr. Colin Carter of the University of California, Berkley. Alberta-raised Carter had co-authored with University of Manitoba's Dr. Al Loyns, a landmark book examining Canada's monopoly grain system. And his court testimony pinpointed again that book's findings that an open market would enhance farmers' returns.

Another witness who brought an unusual depth of experience to court was **Richard Dobranski, who** farms 3520 acres near Roblin, Man., north of Riding Mountain National Park. Dobranski grows wheat, barley and specialty crops. He also has 110 head of cattle and a 75-head bison herd. And he offered some telling insights into how the market works for non-board grains growers can sell themselves.

Dobranski had been a grain marketer/partner in Allstate Grain Co. for some years. Farmers dealt with his old firm voluntarily, he explained. They were offered a variety of choices. They could contract for a fixed price, a floating price or a cash price. And a 'pooling' option was catching on as farmers grew to trust the company. All profits went back to the farmers after expenses such as cleaning and freight were deducted. And the company got a stated-in-advance marketing fee.

Ric had tried a buy-back twice to sell grain to the US. But he was frustrated when the Board levied a storage and interest charge even though the grain had never left his farm.

Grower Brian Otto also testified. A teacher by training, he grows wheat, barley and specialty crops on his 2200 acre farm at Warner, AB. His barley goes for malt and to the local feed market. He said the monopoly prevents him marketing his grain directly to the US when prices are higher there, except under the buy-back. And this was costly to him.

ALMOST A "WHO'S WHO" OF FARM COMMUNITY LEADERS

Chairman Tim Harvie of the Alberta Barley Commission which funded that Charter Challenge farms 907 acres at Cochrane, west of Calgary, growing barley, oats and canola. Most of his grain goes for feed, so to get desperately-needed extra revenue from value-added, he has set up a feed grain rolling enterprise. He delivers rolled grain directly to buyers, often to local feed lots.

Harvie testified that the monopoly's pooling system doesn't reward producers for their top product. Yet his malt barley must go through the board, as well as the wheat and regular barley. He sells his canola "off-board."

Conrad Johnson came from Montana to set up his big 6000-acre spread near Bracken, Sask., in 1975. He grows wheat, durum, barley, lentils, canary seed and oats in what can be a limited rain-fall area. He testified that he and some friends built an "inland terminal" to recover costs that would normally go to the grain trader. His wheat can go up to 17% protein, but he loses out on this because the CWB won't pay a premium for anything over 14.5%.

Ted Cawkwell, who farms 6000 acres near Nutt Mountain, Sask., testified that he grows perhaps 1000 acres of wheat, 2000 of barley, 800 of oats, 850 of peas, and 900-1000 of canola in a four-year rotation.

Yes, this line-up of growers was almost a "who's who" of farmers and community leaders in the Western prairies. Incredibly, all were being targeted by the Ottawa grain monopoly. And in their testimony, they all described the board as inflexible and unresponsive, said it stood in the way of their ability to make full use of their operations. Yet their goal was simple. They didn't want to become Canadian rebels – just to win justice.

National Farmers Union President Nettie Wiebe also came forward to testify, expressing her strongly ideological left-wing bent. Wiebe and her husband farm 2400 acres 70 km southwest of Saskatoon. She has a PhD from the University of Calgary.

Wiebe rejected any loosening of the present monopoly, said she preferred to have the state marketing her grain rather than having to do it herself. In fact, she would prefer Ottawa to extend its monopoly to other crops.

But she said the question of "what is best" for all farmers is a matter for Parliament and not for the courts.

"THE CANADIAN STATE WILL BE DECLARED INCAPABLE..."

With the testimony completed in that Charter Challenge, Judge Muldoon brought down his crucial report. He noted that these growers seed non-board crops which they can sell to advantage for they have ready access to daily market information. He noted that they can produce high quality crops and the CWB doesn't always recognize this, and he admitted growers had cause to criticize the Board operations, and that they wanted the freedom to sell their own grain, confident they could get better prices and profits on their own.

Then he offered a curious statement. If the growers succeeded in breaking the monopoly, "..it will mean the Canadian State will be declared to be incapable of ever again creating such a marketing instrument no matter to whom the people entrust a parliamentary majority, no matter what be the will of Parliament.....(and) The federal power over trade and commerce will be gravely diminished, if not mortally drained."

The judge continually referred to "economic policy," saying "The Charter ought not to protect economic rights...(and) Government should not be hamstrung in developing economic policy, whether in favor of collective or individual rights."

He kept referring to "economic freedom" and seemed to be saying human freedom was irrelevant in this case, that government is the master; the citizen's duty is to do what he is told until Parliament specifies a different route.

"No economic philosophy, either of the 'right' or of the 'left' should ever become constitutionally entrenched by operation of the Charter," he said.

He wrote, "The Canadian Charter of Rights and Freedoms was never intended to be, nor is it an instrument to protect commercial or property rights."

He quoted a '94 study which said "..property did not make it into the final version of the Charter for at least two reasons. First provincial governments and the NDP (more on behalf of the NDP government of Sask. than on behalf of socialism) insisted that it be dropped. The provinces had the major jurisdiction over property and they naturally feared federal judicial interference, especially in the realm of natural resources."

The judge said, "The Charter has never before and still

does not protect economic liberty or property rights."

He wrote, "The plaintiffs have shown that they as individuals could do better on their own."

And the facts are that prairie farmer after prairie farmer today including the many in this book, are making the point daily that their freedom to manage their farms and market their crops is greatly impaired by wheat board interference.

Yet he added, "Parliament's definition of the designated area in no way singles out western Canadian farmers in a manner which negatively impacts their fundamental human dignity or freedom."

Muldoon added, "Common sense shows that the designated area is the principal grain-growing area of Canada. Agronomic equality is not a Charter right."

Yet growers would argue that the issue is human freedom, not 'agronomic equality' whatever that is.

Judge Muldoon also wrote, "The history of the grain economy demonstrates in the evidence before the Court that the free market generates gluts and famines, high prices and low prices, and speculators having taken unconscionable advantage of the grain producers. Moreover the free market forces also generate counter-market production. Canada enjoys a worldwide reputation for non-corrupt reliable marketing of grain."

Yet Muldoon's statement would seem to be totally at odds with that of one politician whose life has examined and lived through this idea. One-time NDP Premier of Ontario Bob Rae expressed his views powerfully in his book, "The Three Questions,"(1998) which seemed to indicate he had faced up to the truth of government monopolies at last.

He wrote, "Fortunately the Marxist experiment has been deeply repudiated in virtually every part of the world. In a manner unthinkable a generation ago, there is literally no major society anywhere that embraces the view that collectivist solutions based on the elimination of significant property right and functioning markets are a better, higher order than some kind of capitalism.

"Investors in Canada can hardly expect less. Surely we don't want governments expropriating property, whoever owns it, without compensation or due process."

Many prairie growers would go further today, and point out that the Soviet Union, with its unlimited market controls, went bankrupt. Its great experiment failed disastrously. And Saskatchewan's economy and that of a good part of the west, languished from a lack of freedom.

In fact most economists know only too well today that a free market, with the personal freedom it provides, offer the only path to a prosperous fulfilling society.

But with Judge Muldoon's report, growers realised they had no choice but to appeal over the heads of ruling politicians and bureaucrats and perhaps even the courts, to the people themselves.

7

IS GRAIN MONOPOLY OTTAWA'S CONTROL LEVER OVER PRAIRIES?

Grower Jim Pallister's tireless research unearthed compelling evidence that Ottawa uses the monopoly as a control lever - that its wheat policy may be even worse than Trudeau's reviled National Energy Program. Martin Luther King's answer in earlier times was, "Break an unjust law openly, lovingly."

OTTAWA'S WHEAT AND BARLEY MONOPOLY WORSE THAN TRUDEAU'S NEP

With so many growers under vicious attack from Ottawa's grain monopoly, Manitoba farmer Jim Pallister could have only one response. He had helped start Farmers for Justice. Now he was among those leading it into the very heart of the struggle to free up growers and the West itself.

This struggle isn't new. Hardly a soul in the west doesn't have nightmares about former Prime Minister Pierre Trudeau's National Energy Program of the 1970's which siphoned off billions of prairie dollars to the east. And Pallister sees Ottawa's wheat and barley laws as perhaps even worse.

For Ottawa never seized ownership of prairie oil and gas. It just taxed them. But it seizes ownership of these grains. And to add insult to injury, some Eastern Canadians who own shipping companies and grain terminals seem to have lined their pockets at prairie farmers' expense. Yes, Pallister likens the monopoly wheat board to the hated National Energy Program of the '70's. He says its ongoing rip-offs of prairie farmers and the prairie economy are too much to bear.

"The Wheat Board Act was brought in as a war measure in 1943 for a simple reason - to see that Canada's allies such as Britain got needed grain at the lowest possible price," says Pallister. "But that subsidy to our allies came right out of the farmers' pockets, not the taxpayers."

Ottawa later made a modest payment to partly compensate growers. But it didn't revoke the Act after the war. And he has found convincing evidence it had a simple and sinister reason. He now believes that grain monopoly enabled Ottawa to extract lots of money from the west.

"In fact the Board and the Crow rates devastated the prairie value-added food industry, robbed the west of numberless jobs and measureless wealth," he says.

Pallister's nature could never accept a continuing role as a victim of politics - especially when it is Central Canada using its overwhelming voting power to keep down the resources-rich west and use those resources for its own purposes. He has criss-crossed the prairies seeking further insights and enlisting allies to the cause.

He has also written dozens of newspaper columns and given innumerable speeches. His telephone bills have soared as he and a growing network of farmers work to keep informed and to wage their struggle.

In fact, no one understands better what Ottawa's stranglehold over growers and the industry really means. That monopoly board is subservient to Ottawa's political strategies and to its wishes. Unlike the legislation that designates the Canada Grain Commission as being "in the interests of farmers," the Wheat Board Act specifies the monopoly is responsible to the Crown and not to growers. No wonder the Board interferes in growers' cropping decisions and denies them the freedom to sell their wheat and barley to the highest bidder. No other farmers in Canada are so blatantly victimised.

SEIZE THE GRAIN, CONTROL THE PRAIRIES!

Pallister's endless digging into the history of this struggle has brought him to one devastating conclusion - one he hesitates, even hates, to say aloud. But he has become totally convinced **the CWB Act is Ottawa's way of controlling the prairie economy.** That's why his simple message rings out, "Its time for every Westerner to stand up and cry, 'Enough is enough!'"

Pallister has plenty at stake. Ottawa's actions hurt over

100,000 farmers who are forced to hand their wheat and barley over to the Board. And fighting to shake free has already cost Pallister $100,000 out of his own pocket. Further, those actions are devastating the west and Canada too. He believes his country is at risk.

In his sleuthing, Pallister went to Alberta historian David Bercuson who had also been researching. Bercuson had dug up correspondence between Ottawa and the North Atlantic Treaty Organisation (NATO) from the mid '50's which told a shocking story. It revealed that Canada offered to build a strategic grain stockpile as a contribution to Cold War defence.

And correspondence among Canada's bureaucrats confirmed that these bureaucrats doubted they could build this stockpile if the grain trade went back into private hands.

In effect, said Bercuson, Ottawa used the monopoly board to seize the farmers' grain as a way to control the prairie economy - and too bad for the farmers. It was the only way to build that strategic grain stockpile. Ottawa got cheap grain it could use in its foreign programs. And it could get away with spending less money buying aircraft carriers and tanks. The strategy brought big savings to eastern taxpayers. Western farmers paid the price. They had to forgo cash flow and build or buy more grain bins.

In effect, the Board's monopoly control over quotas and transportation meant Ottawa didn't have to pay for Canada's NATO stockpile. Growers paid instead.

Pallister remembered vividly the cost on his farm. "We had grain in the garage, in the hayloft, everywhere."

HOW OTTAWA SACRIFICED THE PRAIRIES

That Wheat Board Act had another devastating impact, says Pallister. It enabled Ottawa to keep prairie farmers from adding value to their products.

"Hundreds of privately owned flour mills dotted the prairies before the Board began to confiscate wheat and ship it to Ontario for processing," he recalls. "Over 20 percent of the wheat was milled here. Now we're down to 3 percent."

He holds up a six-page CWB list of these mills that were busy buying and milling wheat and creating jobs and wealth before Ottawa's 1943 policies shut them down. Once they were gone, the government board began shipping that wheat to Ontario and Quebec for processing. The Crow rate helped pay for shipping the grain east. This transferred the jobs and wealth there. And it changed the shape of the prairies and Canada in a thousand ways.

"Consider this," says Pallister. "Growers today might get $4 a Bu. for wheat taken by the Board. But if that wheat could be milled in the west and further processed, its value might reach $20 to $80 per Bu. That would create numberless jobs. It would build prairie towns and cities. And prairie political power too.

"In fact," he says, "if Western growers wrested control of their industry back from Ottawa it would create an economic boom on the prairies.

"Yet it is illegal for a farmer to mill his own wheat here. It is illegal to transfer it, to export it, to buy or sell our own wheat or barley, without first selling it to the Board and then buying it back at a Board-approved price."

He adds with fierce determination, **"This will have to change."**

EXEMPT FROM ACCESS TO INFORMATION LAWS. HAS IT SOMETHING TO HIDE?

In digging into this system, Pallister and others have unearthed some unconscionable facts. Like...the Board is one of only a very few federal agencies exempt from Canada's access to information laws.

"Does this mean the Board has something to hide?" he asks.

He has found mounting evidence that Ottawa continues to undermine the west. When the prairie hog industry was deregulated in 1995, freeing up growers to develop strategies for their own farms and for the industry, the payoff was fast. Big hog farms and new packing plants sprang up, creating jobs and prosperity.

Logic would say that if prairie growers can get control of their own wheat and barley, it would also trigger an economic boom creating new jobs and wealth.

"But Ottawa fears such a development," says Pallister. "The votes are in the East. So it is determined to keep the west producing raw grain. Then Ottawa can direct any value-added boom to Ontario and Quebec.

"That's why prairie farmers are jailed if they try to mill or export or sell their own wheat or barley. They must hand it over to the board."

Yes, the politicians make ringing speeches saying the reason they deny growers their freedom is to see that all growers come out the same. "The great equaliser!" they call it. Or they say growers need protection from the big bad buyer. But Pallister's sleuthing found that story doesn't hold water.

NOT EQUALITY - BUT SWEETHEART DEALS

The monopoly board parades under the guise of equality for all. But look what it does. It enters into sweetheart deals that pay some farmers more than others for their grain. A contract with the United Kingdom miller, Warburton, for instance, pays farmers in a select prairie area $1 per Bu. premium for the same grade of grain on the same day of delivery.

"If the Board is true to its mandate," Pallister asks, "why doesn't it share that $1 premium with all permit holders?"

He calls the Board a 'demockery' because it dictates policy to prairie farmers. Yet in a recent vote 66 percent of Alberta farmers had favoured a dual market system where a grower would be free to sell his own wheat and barley himself if he chooses.

BOARD BLOCKED MALTING BARLEY SALES TO US

Yes, the Board prevents growers from selling their own barley. But when it tries to sell the barley itself, its methods can kill the deals too.

Pallister's research found that malt plants in Jamestown and Fargo, ND, wanted to buy malting barley from Manitoba growers. But growers wanting to make those sales would first have to buy their own barley back from the Board. And that would wipe out any profit, for the Board always sets the buy-back price so high that farmers can't do the deal.

In fact, Board employees admitted in court that only .0004 percent of wheat and barley is sold back to prairie farmers. Growers simply can't compete after paying inflated buy-back prices.

Those malt plants had no choice but to buy the malting barley from the Board. But the Board's methods piled up costs at the farmers' expense. Instead of shipping the grain directly across the border at Emerson, MB, the Board sent it via rail to Thunder Bay. Then it went by lake vessel to Duluth and back inland by rail to North Dakota.

"Every bushel was handled five times," Pallister found. "That cost growers 30 cents per time, or $1.50 per Bu. by the time the grain reached the buyer. No wonder buyers complain about excess handling, peeling, and contamination of malt barley.

"Those maltsters were prepared to send trucks to Manitoba to buy barley right from farmers to ensure quality. But the board's stranglehold prevents it."

These shenanigans make it easy to see why many elevator companies support the monopoly, he says. The Pools, for instance, can make profitable export sales despite their extra elevation costs. They get over 30 cents for every bushel they elevate in the country, another 30 cents when they load it into vessels at the terminal. And they get trucking, storage and administration costs, which growers wouldn't have to pay if they were free.

But these elevator companies aren't adding value - they are subtracting it, because they damage the grain.

Under a free market, says Pallister, buyers could pick up the grain directly from farmers. They'd have quality control and be able to pay growers the savings from reduced handling costs. In fact, US maltsters such as Anheuser-Busch would like to send trucks to Manitoba to buy barley directly from farmers. This would ensure quality and minimal contamination. Even more importantly, millers and maltsters would locate here near the source of high quality grain. But it will never happen as long as the Board has its stranglehold on the prairie economy.

OPEN LETTER TO GOODALE - ARE GROWERS RIPPED OFF?

Pallister asked simple questions in an open letter to Wheat Board Minister Ralph Goodale. Like, why can't the customer just pick up grain right from farmers in Manitoba and Saskatchewan as under a free market? Because it's no secret customers complain about excess handling, peeling and contamination. Then farmers could be paid all the savings from reduced handling costs. And this would transform grain farming.

And he asked, "Is it true that transfer elevators in Montreal and Baie Comeau, Que., get over $1 million of farmers' money from the Board to load each vessel? For if prairie farmers could mill or export their own grain, that money would stay with growers here."

He betrayed a touch of sarcasm when he asked if government policy doesn't seem directed to benefit powerful eastern vested interests with ties to that government? And he went further, stating his profound belief, "Some eastern Canadians who own shipping companies and grain terminals have lined their pockets at prairie farmers' expense."

He asked, "Why do a few influential farmers like seed growers and presidents of farm groups, and advisory committee members - sort of the elite - get export licences for free? With no buyback? Because ordinary growers don't. Does the Wheat Board Act not say everyone has to hand his grain over to the board?"

And he asked, "Why do you allow certain farmers who support your monopoly to get millions of dollars in bonus money direct from buyers? Warburton's and Manitoba Pool, for example, have paid millions to certain farmers. Doesn't all money from export sales have to go into the pool for all to share?

"And when trainloads of grain are hauled across the mountains to the Pacific and then hauled back again and growers have to pay the cost, is that a make-work program at farmers' expense?

"In fact," he asked, "why do you refer to the CWB as 'the farmers' agency' in your speeches and letters to the editor? But in court, you call it 'my agency'? Do you just want farmers to feel they are in control, when really, your government controls them?

"And if the Wheat Board was changed in law to have a duty to farmers, and not just to you, none of these silly but expensive things would continue to go on. Or would they, Mr Goodale?"

The bottom line is that farmers have no legal appeal mechanisms to find out about their business. And Ottawa and the courts make sure this continues.

BOARD APOLOGISTS

Pallister and other growers can cite endless examples of how Ottawa's monopoly costs growers dearly. Apologists for it, and even growers trying to perpetuate this costly system for whatever reason, recite tired clichés. One Manitoba grower repeated for the media the slogan that the board is respected around the world for quality and cleanliness of product and dependability of supply, etc. He was forgetting that the grower is responsible for these qualities.

And he retold the tired old socialist cry that the open market is inefficient - even though study after study in grain has shown the opposite. And a glance at what a free market has done for the US economy, compared to what a command economy has done for Russia, quickly confirms those studies.

This apologist proclaimed that the board moves grain efficiently, yet endless studies have shown the free market is the basis of today's breathtaking world prosperity. And in a sweeping generalisation that would never stand scrutiny, he said Americans don't like the board because it does such a great job for Canadian growers.

One can ask, **If the Board is so good, how come Saskatchewan's population** hasn't risen in 60 years? How come when Wheat Board Minister Charley Mayer moved oats from the board onto the free market, sales to the US boomed - yet the board had always said no market existed there? And why were five new oat processing mills then built on the prairies?

THE MONOPOLY MAY GO, AND THE FUTURE MAY COME, SOONER THAN WE EXPECT

Jim Pallister has drawn one lesson from Ottawa's stubborn refusal to free prairie growers. Most farmers should just forget wheat and barley for a while, he advises. Because the extreme left has control of wheat for export and milling.

Growers will get it back some day, he predicts. And when that day comes, there will be 100 Warburton-type contracts available from companies and new mills that will come in paying them quality-based cash premiums. And that will be far better than getting just one Pool supper.

In fact, he says, companies from all over the world will be at the door of every farmer, one day, with contracts and production opportunities.

Why? That's simple. Thanks to our soil, climate and effort and not to any bureaucracy, Prairie growers produce quality grain. Forget wheat and barley, he says. The Board controls them. Today 80 companies are already here buying our pulses - and acreage is small compared to wheat.

Look south across the border, he urges. The North Dakota Grain Dealers Assoc. has 260 members. And that shows how many Canadian and world companies will come here to bid on our wheat and barley when the monopoly goes.

A change of mindset is needed, says Pallister. Every grower must think of himself as a small businessman or woman, as a trader. Farmers' thinking must be driven by marketing and wealth creation. Then they will make their farms profitable.

Pallister has carefully saved old magazines. And he notices that before the Wheat Board take-over in 1943, those papers were full of solid market and price information for farmers. Then it all changed. Those papers turned to politics - because grain and politics had become one.

A GENERATION OF MARKETING ILLITERATES – "JUST SIT UP AND BEG"

Yes, Ottawa created a generation of marketing illiterates, he says. Growers weren't allowed to sell anything. So why develop marketing skills? "No wonder farm organisations to this day still think their job is to just sit up and beg. If Ottawa has made it illegal to buy, sell or add value, what else can farmers do but ask for handouts?"

In an astounding analogy, Pallister says Ottawa did to farmers in one generation almost exactly what it achieved on Indian reserves. It made them dependent and helpless by taking away their individual property rights and their freedom to trade. "A fascinating similarity," he calls it.

Pallister burned his permit book five years ago when the monopoly started raiding farms, charging and jailing people. He refuses to go through the wheat board at all now. And he says he won't ever use a permit book again. Not until its voluntary. It's a matter of principle.

"ITS LIKE GROWING UP"

He puts all his energy into crops he can sell himself. And in focusing on canola and pulse and other special crops, as well as feed grains, cattle and hogs, look what he and other growers are doing. They are finding rotations they can use without going to wheat.

He names hundreds of small and medium sized companies, and groups like the Canola Council, pulse associations, Winnipeg Commodity Exchange, and so many other institutions of free men and women working together voluntarily. These people and groups are trading, seeking wealth.

"And it works. But of course, nothing else ever has.

"And what a tremendous liberating and empowering feeling. Losing your book, your ID number. I'm not a number. I'm a man. Suddenly a bright world is open to you. A sense of new responsibility is there. And all the opportunity that goes with it.

"It's like growing up. No one holding my hand any more. Like driving out on the land for the first time as a young man all by myself. It's your life to take control of. Try it!" he urges other growers.

BILL CAIRNS GOES TO THE LOCK-UP – REPORTS, "ANDY SOFTENED THEM UP!"

Meanwhile grower Bill Cairns' freedom struggle finally came to a shocking climax and his name returned to the news headlines. Cairns' crime was like that of so many other growers who had been thrown into jail, he refused to allow Ottawa's monopoly to confiscate his grain without a struggle.

The police had grabbed him at the same border crossing as it grabbed Andy McMechan. Their trials concluded in Feb. '96, at the Virden, MB, Courthouse. And the judge pronounced them guilty and levied fines on them.

The Crown appealed, seeking stiffer fines and a jail term. Cairns' fines were more than tripled to $1000 on each of two charges. He faced up to 60 days in jail if he didn't pay.

He refused to concede that Ottawa had the right to seize the grain he grew on his own farm. And he told the judge, "You may as well put me in jail right now because I am not paying the money."

As he faced the music, many farmers had gathered to support him, and their militancy showed only too clearly. Crown Attorney Clyde Bond required a police escort to get through the crowd outside the courthouse.

But finally, in Feb., '97, Cairns heard the jail cell doors

clanging behind him. And he shuddered as they vibrated through every fibre of his body. Yes, his term had begun at the Brandon Correctional Institute where Andy McMechan had already served his time.

WIFE PATRICIA STRUGGLED TO CONTROL HER EMOTIONS

As this agony played out, his wife Patricia struggled to control her emotions. In a massive understatement, she told the media, "It will be tough having him away from home for the next 60 days."

As she gritted her teeth, she revealed the remarkable courage of these angry farm families. She proclaimed that her husband was doing the right thing because the public was getting sick of the government dictatorship. Canadian Farmers for Justice members urged all growers to phone Pat Cairns with words of encouragement.

Like all those growers, Cairns was certain he didn't belong in that jail cell. And he wasn't prepared to bow down to this 'injustice.' This freedom struggle simply had to be won. And now he saw the overwhelming need was to keep the spirits high of all those growers who were continuing the struggle.

His first message from behind bars at the Brandon Correction Institute to growers and the public brimmed with his spirit of confidence and resolve and even humour. "At the end of my first week here in the BCI, (I can say) I have been treated with a lot of respect and interest by both the inmates and the prison personnel.

"Everybody who hears the story of us guys and gals who have been charged find it unbelievable you can be fined and jailed by a system that professes to protect and help farmers."

He added, tongue in cheek, "Here is good news for you fellows who haven't paid your fines. The guards are going to have a new farmers' wing built onto the BCI."

He urged FFJ growers on the outside, "Keep up the good work. We need more meetings and information like you have been putting on. Give 'Em Hell!"

And with a reassuring chuckle, he added, "Andy did a hell of a job of softening everybody up around here. Following him is a piece of cake."

Cairns was inevitably anxious about his livestock at

home on the farm. But wife Pat assured him that neighbours and friends were doing "a terrific job of calving out cows and are getting ready to farrow a bunch of sows for us. I don't know how to thank them enough."

THE TRAGEDY – GROWERS DENIED FREEDOM TO MANAGE THEIR OWN FARMS

A dramatic picture emerges from these profiles. All of these growers put in endless hours creating a future for their families, their communities and the country. The tragedy for them and for all Canada is simple. The government monopoly denies them the freedom to manage their own farms and to build their communities and their country. It has fought fiercely against these farmers whom it is supposed to serve.

How can this have happened? Even as this century was ending, the goal of Ottawa's grain monopoly was clearly to continue treating growers like sheep. That way, it hoped they would continue to take their orders obediently.

But its not turning out to be that easy. These determined growers were learning how to appeal over Ottawa's head to the public itself, convinced that ordinary people would be able to understand.

"TO BREAK AN UNJUST LAW OPENLY, LOVINGLY, SHOWS RESPECT" - KING

And then in Feb., '97, these growers came up with perhaps a stroke of genius. They turned to an earlier moment of world history and focused on one of the most courageous acts ever carried out in North America.

Martin Luther King Jr. had committed his life to perhaps his country's greatest struggle – the fight for racial equality. And this man of God had learned some power lessons. Perhaps the most important was that there might sometimes be no alternative but to challenge an unjust law. And even to break it.

King understood as well as anyone alive the cost of breaking the law. In his Birmingham jail cell in the 1950's, this Baptist minister had pondered the issue endlessly. And in a letter written in that cell, he had phrased it with a simple eloquence that resonated around the world.

He wrote, "One who breaks an unjust law must do so openly, lovingly, and with a willingness to accept the penalty."

King went on, "I submit that an individual who breaks a law that his conscience tells him is unjust, and who willingly accepts the penalty of imprisonment in order to arouse the conscience of the community over its injustice, is in reality expressing the highest respect for the law."

Like Martin Luther King, the prairie growers might well have been breaking the law. Certainly their headline-grabbing border runs caused rage among some politicians and bureaucrats and controversy among farm groups.

But what was the alternative? Simply asking for change didn't work. They knew from bitter experience that only when those laws were changed could they get full market price for their grain. And only then could they pay their bills and continue on their farms.

Like Martin Luther King Jr., those growers desperately wanted to respect the law. That's why they issued an ongoing barrage of news releases to inform the public and the politicians of their plans and their actions. But by holding up King's powerful words they had found perhaps the most effective way of all to drive home their ringing message.

Yet the Ottawa politicians and bureaucrats who were in charge continued to scorn their pleas for freedom and justice.

8

"LIKE THE MANY-HEADED SERPENT IN GREEK MYTHOLOGY"

In Greek legends, when people cut the head off a 'hydra,' two or more heads replaced it. Growers now found in their court battles with the monopoly that like those hydras, "when we finish dealing with one issue, two replace it." Evidence mounts that the monopoly's dictatorial powers aren't authorised by the Act – that those jailings may be illegal. Norm Colhoun's days of agony

28 GROWERS ON TRIAL – LIKE THE MANY-HEADED SERPENT IN GREEK MYTHOLOGY, THE HYDRA

The human drama of that mass border crossing in March, 1996 proved irresistible to the media. Growers were defying Ottawa's monopoly and shouting out their support for fellow-growers Andy McMechan and Bill Cairns who had already been charged. And to add to that drama, 28 growers joined in another high-profile border crossing ten days later. They were charged for this 'crime' and for other crossings some had made that spring.

The public was captivated by these strange events. And it had to ask, Why would these leading citizens deliberately break the law, knowing they would be charged and summoned to court?

These freedom fighters were not naïve. They knew what might lie ahead. They could face weeks or months of costly and agonising preparations for their trials (in fact those months would stretch into years.) Yet they still had to run their farm businesses. And they might finally face jail time.

But now they got a break. Their trials were repeatedly delayed, giving them time to plan and research their case in painstaking detail. And they searched exhaustively into the monopoly board's real legal status, putting it under the microscope as perhaps had never been done before.

POWERFUL LEGAL RULINGS BUILT FORMIDABLE CASE- UN HUMAN RIGHTS BINDING ON CANADA - DICTATORIAL POWERS NOT AUTHORISED BY ACT

Their research paid off with a succession of powerful legal rulings. And now the unthinkable began to emerge. They could find nothing in law compelling them to hand over their grain. When they finally got to court in early 1999, they were convinced of one thing – Ottawa's board lacked the power in law to seize their grain, even though it had been doing this for half a century. They presented compelling evidence it was acting far beyond its power under the Act.

One legal ruling they brought forward said if Parliament intended to expropriate Prairie farmers' grain, the act must clearly state it. And a 1965 case ruling had found, "The CWB Act...does not authorise the CWB to expropriate the wheat and barley grown and owned by producers in the Designated Area (and it) does not state that all wheat and barley grown in (there) must be sold to the Board."

In fact, the Act said, "The board shall...buy all wheat produced in the Designated Area (DA) and **offered** by a producer." But this surely proved their point - if growers don't offer their grain to the board, the board can't sell it.

They also found the Board has power to control the handling and transportation of grain in Canada (for)...orderly marketing. But the Act doesn't say it may expropriate farmers' grain or even that all grain grown in the DA must be sold to it.

And they showed that the courts have found Ottawa may be able to control **officially graded grain. But it can't control non-graded grain. And since t**he grain that those growers exported was ungraded, they were simply transporting their own property.

They called it discrimination that growers outside the Designated Area, such as those in Ontario, could get licenses to sell their wheat and barley anywhere, inside or outside Canada. But prairie growers were denied licences. They could sell only to the monopoly.

And they found the **United Nations Declaration of**

Human Rights which is binding on Canada, seemed to back their case 100%. It states, "Everyone has the right to own property; and no one shall be arbitrarily deprived of his property."

Yet the monopoly board deprived growers of the grain they grew themselves. And this was in violation of this binding international agreement.

In the growers' eyes, these findings made their case air-tight – the monopoly board discriminated against farmers in the 'Designated Area.' When they got to court, their massive challenge to Ottawa would be, **"The CWB has assumed dictatorial powers that have not been authorised to it by the CWB Act."**

The freedom-seeking growers behind this powerful statement included a remarkable cross-section - Boyd Charles, Orlin Hector, Blake Kotylak, Mark Melle, Donald Skoretz, Ivan Sakundiak, Dwight Lischka, Lymand Carpenter, Kerry Ziola, Sheldon Wallin, Devin Raynard, Don Raynard, Kenneth Oberkirsch, David Fedirko, Richard Fedirko, Douglas Domeij, John D. King, Darren Winczura, Robby Shaw, Joey Mizu, Dale Myxlow, Duane Tessier, Arthur Mainil, Stephanie Mainil, Gary Tucker and Norman Colhoun.

ROD FLAMAN STORY – PURPOSE TO DEVISE STRATEGY, NOT WIN JUSTICE

One of those being charged was Rod Flaman whose German heritage, as we have seen, played a powerful role in his upbringing. Flaman's father had instilled in him as a youth the stern doctrine, "Work hard, forget the pay."

But Flaman now had costs to cover. And his perceptive and fertile mind put this case into a fascinating light. "This Department of Justice attack on us is like that many-headed serpent in Greek mythology - a hydra," he explained. "When you cut the head off a hydra, two more heads replace it. In this court battle, when we finish dealing with one issue, two issues replace it. It's an ugly monster and it's growing."

Flaman was now convinced the purpose of this struggle was "..not to win justice, but to devise strategy." He explained, "Justice Department lawyers have refused to do any serious digging. They refused to examine the real issues. They got convictions against David Bryan and Andy McMechan by continually referring to court precedents. They claimed these precedents were similar to the situation facing us. It was the lazy way. But the judges let them get away with it."

As he became convinced Ottawa's monopoly lacked legal power to seize his grain from his Saskatchewan farm, he set out to devise more effective ways to sell his grain in world markets. And he chose to present a personal case to the judge as well.

He was repeatedly asking the monopoly for a licence to export his grain in early '99. But it kept repeating those hallowed words that he must buy his grain back from the board to get a licence. Yes, the only licences he could get were for grain bought from or belonging to the Board.

Flaman didn't mince words. This meant no licences were available for grain grown and owned by farmers, he said. "And this is in direct contradiction of the law and regulations."

These growers were already contending in Court that the actual licence didn't exist in a legal sense – that enabling legislation had never been published in the Canada Gazette.

Said Flaman,"It also appears from my licence applications that even if the licence did exist, it is never granted to producers for their own grain." He added, "As we have always said, the CWB wants to expropriate – and many people call it 'steal' - all wheat grown by producers in the designated area."

He wrote the Board June 19, '99, saying his discussions with board employees indicate, "Unless I am prepared to buy wheat from the Board, this licence application will not be granted."

His answer to the board was unyielding. "I have no intention of either selling this wheat to the Board or buying it back from the Board." He added, "Mr. Silk (Board assistant counsel Andrew Silk) has refused to give any reasons for the denial of this licence and would prefer in fact to deny that he is denying the applications. There is no basis in law for…the so-called buy back..."

THE AGONIES OF DEALING WITH LAWYERS

Getting to this point had been an excruciating journey for all of these growers. And Norm Colhoun later pulled back the curtain on his own frustrations in that agonising legal battle, admitting his faith in Canada's legal system was badly shaken.

"Dealing with lawyers, listening to them change their advice, helped make it an incredible ordeal," he recalled. "One lawyer who wanted to represent us, offered us an hourly rate. We said, 'No. What is the total fee?' He later cited a total fee figure. We said, 'No, forget it.'

"Further strange things kept happening. The lawyers said to us at first, 'You aren't guilty, you haven't done anything.' But their advice was inconsistent."

These growers were soon concerned that their lawyers were being influenced by powerful forces. And they began to realize that governments and the huge wheat monopoly hire a lot of lawyers.

Colhoun was determined to defend himself in court. Yet in one case, "..the lawyer ignored me, wrote to court saying we were all pleading guilty. Yet the truth was that our day in court was already set. I had already signed three forms which said, 'Be in courtroom 210 at 10 a.m. in Winnipeg, Oct. 19, '98.'"

SIX-HOUR DRIVE TO COURT – NOT ANOTHER SOUL CAME

Colhoun recalls, "I made the six-hour drive to Winnipeg but not another soul came. By 11.00 a.m., still no one had arrived. The lawyer had informed them we all pleaded guilty. Yet I hadn't pleaded guilty. I had signed all documents with the Crown prosecutor. So I was to be there."

But it was a wasted trip. Colhoun had to wonder, What was going on? He noted that in another revealing event, grower Darryl Wallin "..got two different transcripts from the same event."

Colhoun now returned to Saskatchewan where he was among those twenty-eight growers charged with exporting without a Wheat Board license. When their case finally came to court in 1999, they continued to insist there was no such thing as a CWB license because legislation requiring it had never been gazetted.

Then these growers got news of another historic happening. Recalls Colhoun, "Manitoba Crown Prosecutor Anne Krahn had stated in Brandon Court on Oct. 18, '99, before Judge MacInnes, essentially the same point we were trying to make – that a CWB license is not a legal instrument because it is not gazetted."

Here was powerful evidence. And the growers facing Provincial Court Judge Bruce Henning in Regina requested that he take this into account. The judge refused, said the growers could bring that out in the appeal

The growers had also unearthed an Act which seemed to confirm again their point that a person can't be convicted "..if the law hasn't been gazetted."

The end to this phase of the case finally came in sight when Judge Henning informed growers that both sides would complete their arguments in late March, '99 and he would then rule. But the growers faced those days with anxiety – they had been told they faced a maximum penalty of six months in jail and a $50,000 fine each, if convicted.

UP-BEAT GROWER'S EMOTIONS BREAK THROUGH - HE WEEPS

Norm Colhoun had been waiting for three years for this moment to arrive. The former world-circling jet pilot who now farmed and operated a crop spraying business gave his summary talk to the judge on March 24. And once he had delivered his case and made his plea, he let his emotions break through. This normally up-beat and tough grower broke down and wept in front of the court, the judge, the farmers and others there.

Then he reached into his pocket and drew out his auction sale sign for his farm, which was now in danger of being a casualty of his long battle.

"I am going to sell it," he told the judge. "If I had focused on farming instead of freedom for the last three years, this wouldn't be."

Later, he left no doubt where he stood. "This can't be democratic in any way. They can throw as many new curve balls as they want. But eventually they must face up to the facts. According to the law, we are innocent. We must be freed. Eventually we will win."

(As it turned out, Norm and Laurie Colhoun's agonizing ordeal seeking justice in the courts lasted nearly five years. But in Dec., 2000, a Manitoba Court of Queen's Bench justice threw out three of four Canada Customs Act charges against him and withdrew the fourth. Explained Colhoun, "I've been trying for the last 4 ½ years to get disclosure from the Crown and they said I had full disclosure. Then on the first day of the trial they handed over four sets of disclosure." Norm and Laurie could finally breath easy once more.)

WOULD GROWERS LITIGATE TO RECOVER LOST MONEY?

Soon grower Rod Flaman was raising the stakes even higher. He wrote, "It amazes me that after 50 plus years there has not been a judicial review of this procedure."

He warned this could change very soon. "A judicial review is exactly what I plan to pursue if this licence is not granted."

He pressed home his point in a letter to wheat board employee Trevor Magee. "As you can also imagine, Mr. Silk and yourself will be called to testify in the proceeding..(and)..if there is a judicial review, I would expect a ruling that the CWB buy-back policy is illegal."

In case anyone thought he was speaking only for himself, Flaman added, "If that happens, the CWB might find that numerous individuals would commence litigation for financial losses going back many years. The potential losses to the CWB in this scenario would be considerable and real."

Just how considerable one could only speculate. But even that might not be difficult. The story in this book documents losses suffered by a few prairie growers who are denied their freedom to sell their own grain. Those losses have come to $50,000 or $100,000 or more for a single grower for a single year.

Extend that figure to the tens of thousands of growers, and extend it for 5 years or 10 years or more. Losses could be astronomical. If growers sued to recover them, could Ottawa's resources handle such damages? Certainly the Wheat Board couldn't. But Ottawa and the Wheat Board are one.

Canada's taxpayers might shudder at those massive costs.

"Alternatively," said Flaman, "if the Board grants export licences as in my current application, its losses will be either negligible or fictitious."

WHEAT BOARD LACKS POWER TO SEIZE GRAIN

Flaman waited endlessly for a decision on his court case. But he had no intention of quitting. When he learned that Wheat Board directors were meeting in Winnipeg on July 8 and 9, '99, he faxed a letter to the Board office asking that each director be given a copy of it before the meeting.

In that letter, he laid out his case again. And he added that his research revealed the CWB Act requires all growers in Canada be treated the same on licence applications. So why was he being treated differently because he farms in the prairies? He just wanted fair treatment - a no-cost licence to export his grain, like growers in the east get.

He added, "Mr. Trevor Magee of the Board has stated under oath in Court on numerous occasions that these licences are always issued on a no-cost basis and that this policy is uniformly applied in all parts of Canada."

FLAMAN IN DEADLY EARNEST

Flaman was in deadly earnest. He went on, "International sales are pending upon this licence application."

And he cautioned, "Please be forewarned that I will suffer serious financial losses if the Application is denied, and I am forced to sell this high quality American variety of dark northern spring wheat in the domestic Canadian feed market."

He hoped this couldn't happen. But if it did, "I will hold the CWB and its directors responsible. And I will seek restitution in the Courts along with costs and damages."

This was an all-out battle to inform the public. And he made no secret of his resolve. He sent copies of his letter to Lorne Nystrom, MP, and to Lorne Scott, MLA, and to Wheat Board Minister Goodale as well as to the Western Wheat Growers Association, the Barley Growers Association, the Farmers For Justice, the Canadian Taxpayers Federation, the Reform Party and the Saskatchewan Party.

How costly has this episode been for Flaman and the other growers?

"With 'forfeitures,' Justice now wants about $40,000 from me," he said. "We are appealing it all, of course."

And that says nothing of the time and expense he has devoted to his battle. "If they finally come and arrest me and haul my truck away, so be it," he shrugged. "The fight is a long way from over. My truck is only worth about $8,000. So if they want it..."

Flaman's ordeal has convinced him the issue is not justice, its control. "In hindsight," he says, "we growers set out to fight the CWB and wound up fighting the justice system. WE made a mistake and got put on defence. And you can't score that way.

"Now we are turning that around. I want to keep the Justice system/wheat board people on defence. I am going to challenge them on two issues – the alleged monopoly, and the arbitrary and discriminatory refusal to grant me a license.

"The prosecutors will have no court precedent to work on with either of these. I think we will win."

Finally, after 3½ years of court proceedings, the judgement came down on Nov. 22. And in a major sense, it was a shattering blow to the growers. They were found guilty in Regina provincial court of illegally exporting grain.

Judge Bruce Henning handed out small fines - $500 each for failing to get export licences and $1 for not placing their seized grain trucks in custody.

Yet from the growers' viewpoint, the vital principle had been lost. They left no doubt they would appeal to the Supreme Court.

FLAMAN SEEKS $277,000 DAMAGES AND COSTS IN ACTION AGAINST MONOPOLY

Meanwhile Flaman pressed on with his initiative. True to his word, he launched an action in late 1999, and in his statement of claim, named all directors of "the new Canadian Wheat Board Corporation..." as Defendants.

He noted that he had "requested a license to export 9000 bushels of wheat to the United States on May 7, 1999. .....An application form was received by the Plaintiff...on May 12, 1999, which was completed and returned to the new Canadian Wheat Board Corporation.

"The plaintiff has been unable to determine through correspondence with the (CWB.....how) the licence fee would be determined."

He added, "The Plaintiff has refused to offer his wheat for sale to the new (CWB).....thereby putting himself in the same position as a producer outside the designated area who by law is not able to offer his grain for sale to the new (CWB).

Flaman asked for "Punitive damages of $250,000, and Liquidated damages of $27,000 on the sale of the grain. And costs of the action. And any other remedy which this Honourable Court considers appropriate and just..."

Frustrated Lumsden, SK., grower Barry Colhoun and wife Laurie mounted a huge sign on their grain truck crying out their FARMERS FOR JUSTICE message to the public, **"CANADA - THE ONLY COUNTRY IN THE FREE WORLD WHERE FARMERS ARE JAILED FOR SELLING THEIR OWN GRAIN."** It demanded of Wheat Board Minister Ralph Goodale, **"RESPECT AN INDIVIDU-AL'S RIGHT TO MARKET HIS OWN CROPS."**

Grower Dave Bryan, flanked by lawyers Art Stacey (left) and Scott Ellson, of the big Winnipeg law firm Thompson, Dorfman and Sweatman, in court fighting his case in 1998.

Hundreds of angry prairie growers converged on the Saskatchewan Legislature, Regina, in July '99, to protest their lack of freedom to manage their farms and market their own wheat and barley. This parade of tractors, combines, grain trucks, proceeds along Albert St. to the Legislature.

Growers with their farm machines jammed the front of the Saskatchewan Legislature in a display to grab media attention, send their message across the country.

Growers Rod Flaman from Edenwold, SK., addresses the crowd in a cry to government to free up growers to manage their farms and sell their own grain.

At David Bryan's court case in Winnipeg, Feb. '98 (right to left) David Bryan and wife Karen, and growers Carl Ostberg, Dominion City, MB., and John Husband, Wawota, SK.

Grower supporters at Dave Bryan's court case in Winnipeg take time out for lunch – Bill Bell, Deloraine, MB., Bernie Sambrook, Medora, MB., Alex Herle, Neilburg, SK., Delory Nestibo, Wascada, MB.

A few of the growers and wives who were in Winnipeg to support David and Karen Bryan on David's court case.

Gordon Brooks in a beautiful crop of durum wheat on his Belle Plaine, SK., farm. But Ottawa's monopoly seizes the wheat when it comes out of his combine, denies him the freedom to sell it to waiting buyers, or to join with other growers to build a pasta plant and get the benefits of value-added. The monopoly directs the grain to whatever market it chooses.

9

COURT RULES BRYAN DOESN'T OWN THE GRAIN HE GROWS!

The court ruling against Dave Bryan offered every Canadian an astounding insight...that long-running struggle by prairie growers to win freedom to sell their own grain was more than just an issue for the lightly populated West. All Canadians lack property rights. This issue goes to our country's heart

"A HELL OF A PILE OF MONEY"

David Bryan's cash returns on his 2,000 hectares of farm land in the mid 1990's were simply inadequate. But like so many other growers, he was already looking intently across the US border at a beckoning sight – an extra dollar a bushel if he could just sell his grain there.

"Get that dollar into your own pocket and it would be perhaps $50,000 a year on most farms," he explains. "A hell of a pile of money!"

Like every family farmer, when 37-year-old Bryan is managing his farm at Central Butte, 80 km NW of Moose Jaw, he must be in deadly earnest. He and his wife Karen were raising five children. Paying the bills demanded serious decision-making. Access to those US market prices could be the difference between a decent living and a poor one. Or even bankruptcy. He was prepared to fight for the right to sell his wheat and barley there.

That struggle catapulted his name into the news. And now he is one of thousands of prairie growers committed to that furiously controversial idea that marketing their crops should not be an exercise in politics. They are naive enough to think if you grow a bushel of grain you should be able to sell it to whomever you like - probably to the highest bidder.

NO HOT-HEAD – DRIVEN BY SEARCH FOR FREEDOM

Dave Bryan was an early recruit to Canadian Farmers for Justice. But he is no hothead. His every act is planned and deliberate. By nature, he is a thinker. He is just as comfortable reading books like Russian-American philosopher Ayn Rand's 'Capitalism – The Unknown Ideal,' as growing a crop of wheat.

In fact, in this all-important struggle, he wasn't driven by anger but rather by a determination to gain freedom for himself and for others. He was among those 39 growers who rallied to Andy McMechan's support in those March, 1996 crossings and were charged. He remembers only too vividly those events.

"We were just doing him a favour. Andy has land on both sides of the border. We were hauling it from his Manitoba bins to his North Dakota bins.

"It was a muddy day. We hauled the barley past stop-sign waving Canada Customs officers into the US and then we dumped it into Andy's bins. We stayed overnight in Mohall, ND.

"But when we returned to the border, our trucks were seized by Canada Customs. Then we had to take them about a mile up the highway where we were stopped by the RCMP and charged with theft over $5000 for taking them from Customs. We were released on condition we not re-offend – we couldn't go within 10 km. of the Can.-US border, or have contact with any customs officer."

Bryan shows remarkable cool when he looks back at those strange events. No sign of rage flickers on his face when he recalls, "This border truck seizure and what followed was all pre-planned and deliberate. It was orderly. The Customs and the RCMP officers were just doing their jobs. And we truckers were respectful of them.

"We wanted to get the charges into court so we could demonstrate to the public the law's absurdity. This would put political pressure on Wheat Board Minster Goodale."

"A RIGHT, BY ITS NATURE, CAN'T BE VOTED ON"

Over a year later, in mid '97, the struggle continued to grab headlines. These growers were planning another border crossing. And they urged others, "Please join us as we break the control of Incompetence over our industry and over farmers. Come to North Portal on July 15, at 10.00 a.m."

They billed it as the largest border run so far - the 'Andy 500.' The goal was to have 500 trucks take part. Over 100 growers had soon signed on.

But now, Ottawa's ruthless vendetta was having its impact. More than 100 growers had already been charged in border crossings. Some had been jailed and fined thousands of dollars. These and others were becoming hesitant - fearful of the punishing fines and legal costs Ottawa was slamming at them. They were beginning to seek other methods of waging their battle.

With that Andy 500 now proving to be unrealistic, these growers called a rally for Regina where Reform and Saskatchewan Party politicians would bring progress reports on the freedom struggle. And growers could symbolically fill bags of grain and parade for the media, expressing their rage at Wheat Board Minister Goodale. About 425 farmers shut down their combines to attend.

As these events unfolded, Dave Bryan continued to focus on principles rather than short term political gains. Growers were now being asked in votes and surveys for their views on this. Their response was to demand freedom to market their own grain. But Bryan spoke out leaving no doubt he disdained these votes. He explained why in a news release.

"A right, by its nature, can't be voted on," he insisted. "If a majority can vote away a right, then it isn't a right. The individual's right to free trade, his right to property, and arguments about 'rule of law' have captured the hearts and minds and sympathy of Canadians.

"It is this public sympathy that will eventually get Ottawa to allow the courts to protect our individual rights." This was the issue on which growers must wage their battle.

AN ACT OF INDESCRIBABLE COURAGE

It is David Bryan's nature to be quiet-spoken and low key. And on important issues, he is deadly serious. Now, he made a memorable decision. He chose to step forward himself - to back up his words with dramatic action.

But first, he sat down with his 9- and 6-year old sons for a remarkable family conference - one those boys will never forget. He addressed them with wise and memorable words: "Sometimes its necessary and right," he explained, "for good people to willingly go to jail to expose an injustice."

Then in an act of indescribable courage, Dave Bryan hooked his Freightliner truck to its 40-foot grain trailer, loaded it with hard red spring wheat, and set off on his own border crossing. It was July 14, 1997.

The news that he was making the crossing without an export permit flashed across the prairies. His truck cellphone began ringing with calls from the media. His drive became a prairie news story. He crossed into North Dakota and continued a few miles south to Bottineau. Grain buyers there were glad to get his grain. They said they would take more.

SENSE OF SOLEMN DIGNITY MADE IT ALL WORTHWHILE – A LAW HE KNEW WAS WRONG

He recalled later, "When I dumped my load, I was overwhelmed by the sense of solemn dignity that came over me. It came from exercising my right to sell the wheat I grew to whom I chose.

"Those who get the opportunity to experience this emotion won't need to wonder what motivates men to fight for freedom and their right to own their property."

He added, "Many of us had gone to enormous trouble trying to end the grain monopoly. The reward for our efforts could be summed up in this one emotion – the sense of doing what is right. And this made it all worthwhile."

North Portal is a busy 24-hour crossing point. Bryan drove back there from Bottineau and stopped at the border station in Saskatchewan. He told the Customs officer he had hauled wheat into the US without an export license.

Yes, he had been through all this before. But not alone as he was now. Yet he remembers vividly, "The officers were cordial and they were just doing their jobs enforcing the Customs Act." But he was arrested for failing to come to a full stop, and also charged with obstructing justice and assault with a weapon – his truck.

It was a strange event. "Two burly RCMP officers walked in, asked me if I intended to take my truck even though it was under seizure by Canada Customs. I answered, 'Yes.' One of them with whom I had been talking pleasantly, said I would not be allowed to take it without paying the $2,000 fine – that I would be charged with theft.

"Then his eyes started to well up with emotion - he was an officer who had to enforce a law he knew was wrong. I was not a real criminal and he knew it. I was simply a farmer trying to sell my own wheat.

"And worse. I wasn't belligerent or blaming him for seizing my truck. I knew he was just doing his job, as I was doing mine. He was as much a victim of the situation as I was.

"In fact, his job was a lot harder than mine - I would have no trouble sleeping at night. He would."

"I COULDN'T SCRATCH IF I GOT AN ITCH"

Bryan was unable to retrieve his truck so he phoned his wife Karen. She made the five-hour drive to pick him up and drive him home. The next day he loaded up another truck and notified Customs he was returning. And again he was ignoring the buy-back.

Radio stations jumped on the story once more, keeping the prairie audience updated on his progress. At North Portal, he drove through despite some gestures from the RCMP and Customs. At Bottineau, ND, he took a motel room for the night. He dumped his load the next morning, and headed back for the border.

Customs was ready for him. The crossing was blocked off with police cars. Officers told him his truck would be seized. He was handcuffed, shown into the rear seat of the cruiser, read his rights, and he was on his way to the RCMP Detachment at Estevan. It was his first experience in handcuffs, and he remembers vividly the discomfort.

"I couldn't scratch if I got an itch," he said.

He was soon on his way to Winnipeg and that 1000-km ride took about eight hours. Like any common criminal, he was placed shoeless into a cell there to await a court appearance. When he appeared in court, he twice turned down an offer of cash bail of $25,000. And he refused to get a lawyer. "I knew I hadn't done anything wrong and in the end I would be exonerated.

"They asked what I would do if I was convicted. I said I didn't care, that I would continue to haul my grain across the border. I had a moral right to do this and an obligation to my family, my creditors and my bank to conduct my business in a way that would best fulfil those obligations."

But he also refused to give in to anger. Most of the RCMP officers he met "..were friendly and intelligent people," he explained.

He now got the devastating news that the Crown was throwing the book at him. Customs alleged he had failed to come to a full stop at a sign at North Portal, Sask. And it not only charged him with exporting illegally, but also, with obstruction of a Customs officer, dangerous driving, assault with a weapon (his truck) and more.

He was stunned that he was going to face criminal charges as well as charges of exporting without a license. He believed the Wheat Board was behind all this, with Customs doing its dirty work.

HOPING SOME MUD WOULD STICK

"Laying all those charges was like throwing mud at a wall hoping some of it would stick," he said later. He was convinced it was an attempt to intimidate him into pleading guilty to something. Ottawa's politicians and bureaucrats were desperate to somehow get this bothersome matter of freedom for farmers behind them.

"If this wasn't a deliberately engineered entrapment, it was damn close to it," he said.

The growers now issued a news release with the grim news that Bryan had been arrested. And it caught the surrealistic nature of these events. It waxed almost lyrical as it reported, "Customs officials, doing their impression of Northern Border guards, tried to prevent a Canadian citizen from leaving the country...It appears that it is a crisis in this country to do so while carrying food."

Five days after his arrest, Bryan was still being held in Winnipeg Remand Centre. Growers reported in a news release, "He apparently drove past the border guards at...1 or 2 mph. He is in jail on principle...And at a bail hearing...he told the judge he was likely to keep selling his own product and if that made him a dangerous criminal, perhaps he had better be locked away."

Growers had now formed another group, the Canadian Free Enterprise Network (CFEN) to mount a massive support program for Bryan. Its first job was to build a war chest full of money. One of its key spokesmen was the articulate and energetic Rosetown, Sask., grower Russell Larson. That program paid off, raising tens of thousands of dollars. And now, growers had two organisations continually communicating with the farm community and beyond.

One news release summed up the sorry situation. "A brave man. (Bryan's) name now joins the Honour Roll of farmers who've been in jails fighting Canadian Communism. He passionately believes in the right of prairie farmers to market their own grain. And on his own, he is taking on the Liberal government which has been treating the West like a colonial backwater.

"For years Wheat Board propaganda pretended it has been looking out for the growers' best interests, all the while paying them less than world prices. Bryan and FFJ believe it's time to expose the fraud and rot in grain marketing."

"HEAD GAMES" TO BREAK DOWN PRISONERS "ALMOST HUMOROUS" - TWO VISITORS TO HIS JAIL CELL

Bryan's nature is to continually try to discern the reasons behind people's actions. And now he got one more insight. "When a person is in custody it is standard procedure for the police to do everything they can psychologically to break him down, to make him confess his crime.

"Once I figured out the 'head games' they played, their tactics became almost humorous," he recalls. Often times, when an officer was going at him, ".they hoped I would break down. But both he and I knew it was all a crock."

Bryan soon had two visitors in his jail cell - special investigators from Revenue Canada who had already tried to intimidate him into respecting Wheat Board regulations, ".by seizing my truck."

He recalled, "They had also attempted to shame me by laying criminal charges, and putting me in jail. They told me I would be convicted of breaking the Customs Act. But I threw it back in their faces, told them the CWB Act was ridiculous law and it was morally wrong and absurd to try to prevent a farmer from selling his own grain."

Bryan was released from Winnipeg jail on July 21 on $5000 bail and his trial was set for Aug 20 in Winnipeg. Under terms of his bail release, he could not export wheat or barley without a valid CWB export license. And he wasn't allowed to go within 10 km of the Can.-US border or have contact with any customs officer.

BRYAN HIRES TOP LAWYER – SETS PROPERTY RIGHTS AS THE ISSUE

Events were now piling up on this young farmer. His case was set to start in provincial Court in Winnipeg in late August and he also faced charges in courts in Estevan, Sask., and Brandon Man. for other runs made "..to test Canada's blurry grain export laws."

He faced a battle with the entrenched Liberal government and the awesome power of Ottawa's bureaucracy. And with so much at stake, he made another decision. He finally agreed to get a lawyer.

Judge Charles Newcombe in Winnipeg welcomed that decision because "..some of the issues that are going to be raised make me scratch my head." He delayed the case until Bryan could be prepared.

Bryan acted carefully but quickly, retained prominent but youthful lawyer Art Stacey of one of Winnipeg's largest law firms. He soon filed notice that the central trial issue would be property rights. Western farmers were being denied the right to sell their grain - a fundamental right of ownership. Instead, they were forced to submit it to expropriation by Ottawa.

"Could any issue be more important in a free country?" he asked.

This was a Charter Challenge. And Bryan intended to ask that ultimate question - Will the court uphold a farmer's inherent right to own the grain he grows? For if he owns the grain, surely he has the right to sell it where he chooses.

These Free Enterprise Network growers agreed with him that in a free country, no issue could be more important. They were confident they could raise needed funds.

They would put everything into the struggle and stand behind him all the way.

MONOPOLY THREATENS LAW FIRM, "DON'T TAKE US ON"

It shaped up as an awesome battle. The Crown left no doubt it was ready, warning lawyer Stacey it had unlimited budget to protect the Board's entrenched 55-year-old monopoly. This was evidence enough for Bryan that Ottawa would stop at nothing to win – that on any matter on which government feels strongly, it will do whatever it feels is necessary to prevail.

Said Bryan later, "This issue is bigger than any of us first thought. It is about the protection of property rights for all Canadians - the right to own and dispose of our own property without fear of arbitrary expropriation by the federal government...and it deserves to be fought with the best resources available."

Meanwhile the trial date for this strange and unorthodox case was continually being set back.

SURVEY CONFIRMS – US PRICES HIGHER

The most relentless of all growers in seeking the root causes of these injustices was perhaps CFFJ leader Jim Pallister. And he now announced the findings of a once-a-month survey of North Dakota elevators which confirmed everything growers were fighting for. For red spring wheat, the highest posted prices averaged for the year, and the ND averages, were 26% higher than CWB prices. And they were 18% higher for durum, 58% higher for feed barley and 5% higher for malt barley.

Pallister found current prices confirmed this huge difference - durum was bringing over $8 Cdn., FOB Bottineau, in early Sept., '97, reflecting world market prices. Prairie growers could get these prices in their pockets if Ottawa wasn't confiscating their grain. He predicted more and more growers would test Ottawa's will by running grain into the US in the coming fall. And growers would then be in court all over the prairies.

OTTAWA'S BUYING MONOPOLY JUST A FRONT

Now startling new information burst onto the scene. Respected Alberta scientists/journalists, Dr. David Bercusson and Dr. Barry Cooper were also researching this issue. And new findings convinced them Ottawa's buying monopoly and its export control system were really just a front. In fact, Ottawa had a totally different purpose. And a sinister one indeed. Its real purpose was to confiscate Western Canadian private property.

This startling news from such a high profile team offered new hope to Bryan and the farmers' cause. The growers had their eyes focused firmly on the publicity spinning off from these events. The media coverage could have a massive impact on the public's perception of this struggle, driving home the message that the growers were victims of a devious and devastating game. And they simply wanted justice, nothing more.

To win further media coverage, CFFJ urged farmers, "Share your stories. Send in stories of Wheat Board abuses of the buy-back, of licenses, or anything else, to Farmers For Justice."

AN AWESOME $150,000 FUND-RAISING CAMPAIGN TO CHALLENGE OTTAWA'S RIGHT TO "CONFISCATE"

Legal battles are fuelled by money. And Bryan's need for cash to finance his appeal was critical. A lone farmer could hardly raise enough funds for such a battle. So CFFJ growers **(20 Sept, 97,) set up a series of** information/fund-raising meetings in Saskatchewan.

It began on the big-farm-audience Jack Dawes Open Line radio show out of Yorkton, Sask., on Oct. 14. This was followed by a meeting with area farmers at Norquay, and then at a country school house evening meeting at Wawota. Another was scheduled at the Regina Flying Club for Oct. 15, then one at Mary's restaurant at Milestone on Oct. 18, followed by a lunch in Regina with area farmers and a 7.00 p.m. meeting at Rosetown.

With those public meetings and a telephone campaign, Bryan and other growers pulled off a near miracle. They raised nearly $150,000.

Meanwhile a new survey sent growers' spirits soaring. The Canadian Federation of Independent Business had asked, "Should the CWB be reformed to allow farmers a choice in who markets their grain?" The response was 60.2% yes in Manitoba, 62.3% in Saskatchewan. Winnipeg voted 58.9% yes, Regina 66.7% and Saskatoon 70.7% yes. These stunning results showed the public was massively on side with these growers.

"MORE FREEDOM THROUGH LESS GOVERNMENT"

Bryan and his supporters now focused all their energies on the upcoming Constitutional challenge. It would be a landmark case - the most important test ever mounted of the monopoly's legality.

Bryan and lawyer Art Stacey and Manitoba grower Jim Pallister now headed for Calgary to discuss strategy with several key groups. They talked to the National Citizen's Coalition which was helping to finance their struggle, and whose motto, "More freedom through less government," perfectly fitted their own goals. They also consulted with the Property Rights Research Institute. And with lawyers who had argued a Charter of Rights case for the Barley Commission against the Board monopoly.

All agreed Bryan's case was straightforward - he had a good chance. "Focus strictly on the main issue," they advised. "The monopoly is an expropriation by the Federal government and is a violation of farmers' property rights."

Certainly this case was simply the tip of the iceberg. One prairie-wide breakdown in early '98 showed over 260 trucks had now been seized. And prairie courts were dealing with 219 cases involving about 100 farmers charged with selling grain across the border without a CWB permit.

BRYAN PUTS THE GROWERS' CASE

Bryan was charged with four counts under the Customs Act, of trucking 1000 Bu. of barley across the border without a CWB export license, and his case was to start in Winnipeg Feb. 9, '98.

Fellow-grower Jim Pallister dared to be optimistic. Writing in Grainews, he noted that Bryan had an able young lawyer and he had put together a powerful case. He had superb witnesses including a historian/journalist to reveal the true story behind those monopoly powers; highly respected economist Dr. Al Loyns; and an agronomist to show that prairie farmers have no choice but to grow wheat or barley and give it to the monopoly.

He also had a farmer who couldn't mill her grain without handing over title to the monopoly, then buying it back; a farmer who couldn't export without doing the same; and farmer/entrepreneur Glenn Pizzey who had built a flourmill on his Angusville, MB, farm despite the risk inherent in the monopoly's rules.

Pallister gave Bryan an excellent chance of ending the grain monopoly.

In Court, Bryan's goal was an all-out challenge of Ottawa's right to "confiscate" growers' grain, which he said encroached on property and civil rights and breached the Canadian Bill of Rights.

Grower Glenn Pizzey testified how his decision to put in a flour mill had brought him endless grief. The monopoly's rules wouldn't allow him to move his grain across his own farmyard from his bins to the flour mill without giving up ownership. In fact, he had to haul it to town and sell it to the Board. Then he could buy it back at an arbitrarily-set higher price and haul it home to his mill. On one occasion, the bureaucrats told him he couldn't even do that because there was no quota.

In his testimony, Bryan looked back to the beginning. He described the dramatic change in conditions since the compulsory Board was created in war time. The board was continued when the war crisis required Ottawa to take control of various 'strategic' resources.

And finally he asked, "Do farmers own the wheat and barley they grow or does someone else own it?" He insisted Ottawa has no power under the Constitution to lay the charges because the legislation is out of its jurisdiction.

A BLOCKBUSTER RULING - OTTAWA CAN SEIZE ANYBODY'S HOME OR LAND OR RRSP

With the evidence in, Justice James Smith of Man. Court of Queen's Bench brought down his ruling Feb. 21, 98. And it was one more blow to the growers.

He said Ottawa can in fact, force farmers to sell their grain through the board even if this infringes on their civil rights. And he ruled the Ottawa monopoly has "no duty of care to farmers." In fact, "The right to 'enjoyment of property' is not a constitutionally-protected fundamental part of Canadian society."

The answer was, "No!" Justice Smith found Bryan guilty on five charges under the Customs Act, gave him a 2-year suspended sentence and ordered him to pay $9,000 in fines. He threw out Bryan's Constitutional Challenge. The hopes of these many growers were dashed.

But rather than capitulate, Dave Bryan pressed on. He took his case to the Manitoba Appeal Court. And almost a year later, on Jan. 23, '99, he appeared in Winnipeg again.

He said the case "..goes to the heart of property ownership." And he wanted the Court to overturn his Feb. '98 conviction in Winnipeg for violating the Customs act when he hauled grain across the border without a permit.

Again he was denied. The three Court justices ruled Bryan's case was seriously flawed – that the Board's only mandate is to provide "orderly marketing" on behalf of the Federal government.

Lawyer Stacey said this decision appeared to be the first time an appeals level court has declared the property rights of Canadians are totally unprotected.

BRYAN'S HARSH CONVICTION – DOES A FARMER OWN THE GRAIN HE GROWS?

Bryan's terse response was, "You will never build Saskatchewan or the prairie breadbasket with such nonsense."

He called the monopoly an abuse of his property rights for a simple reason. The 1960 Canadian Bill of Rights sets out the constitutional right of every Canadian to control his own property. Yet the monopoly ignored that. It forced him to submit his grain to expropriation by Ottawa

Yes, this freedom search had been side-tracked again. The Bill of Rights had been largely superseded by the Trudeau 1982 Charter of Rights and Freedoms, which lacked property rights.

This devastating ruling offered every Canadian a stark insight into how the country works - and for many, it stood simple common sense on its head. It also came down like a sledgehammer on Bryan. It was the full force of Canada's legal system slammed against a prairie farmer and his family trying to make a living in grain.

Bryan and a growing army of farmers were discovering again that Canada's administered grain system doesn't serve their interests – that the monopoly operates by violating their property rights.

That ruling left no doubt - the growers' long battle for freedom to sell their own grain was more than just an issue for the lightly populated prairies which have been largely ignored for decades. It wasn't simply a 'farmer' issue - it was a freedom issue affecting every Canadian. `

Bryan extended that ruling's dubious logic. "If the Federal Government Board can take my grain without any duty whatsoever to me or any farmers...that's confiscation of private property." He pressed the issue further, said property rights are totally outside Ottawa's jurisdiction.

But this conviction failed totally to bring him to his knees. "Just one more bump in the road," he called it. "In fact a small step of progress. We've finally gotten a court to declare unequivocally that the federal government can come in and seize anybody's home or land or RRSP...any time it wants to."

He was certain of one thing. No free country could allow that to stand. In a statement bristling with logic, he said, "When a grower's grain comes out of his combine, who can deny it is property? It is only common sense he should be able to sell it. If Ottawa can come in and trample on property rights any time it wants, what protection does that provide anybody?"

He appealed that ruling to the Supreme Court where he would be taking on the cream of the country's jurisprudential crop. National Citizens Coalition said it would support him.

"DON'T PORTRAY ME AS A VICTIM"

Bryan is determined the true story of these events must get out to the public. And he found that some journalists covering the story "..wanted to say that I believed the big bad government had put a poor but noble farmer in jail because he tried to buck an 'evil' system.

"This premise is wrong," he insists. "The system wasn't some big evil conspiratorial entity that was there to bilk the poor farmer. It was there because of a bad philosophy and bad economics. Farmers had accepted these ideas when they thought there was some economic advantage in it. I didn't want anyone to think farmers didn't deserve a big part of the responsibility for this Wheat Board monopoly mess."

Bryan goes further and explains, "I didn't want to be portrayed as a victim. There was no sacrifice in it for me. The number of days or weeks I might spend in prison were nothing compared to the goal I was setting out to accomplish. I wanted to contribute to a better future for my family and myself by demonstrating that under current law, farmers didn't have ownership of their own grain."

BRYAN'S NEW CELEBRITY STATUS

But Bryan also carried the struggle to another level. He was invited onto the big-audience Dave Rutherford radio show in Calgary in Feb. '99. There he and the host turned to the real issue - human rights. What did this new finding that Canadian law lacks human rights legislation, really mean?

Host Rutherford let his imagination run, said it means the state has the power to put a highway through your yard if it wants.

The two discussed prairie Canada's catastrophic failure in recent decades to process its grain at home – its failure to produce value-added products like pasta and flour. And its failure to create jobs and wealth. And Rutherford's audience listened.

This battle has been no joy ride for the young farmer. He has spent endless hours preparing his case, and more long hours in the courthouse. Said one observer, "He will now be just as familiar with the long benches in those court rooms as he is with the long rows of grain on his own farm."

Bryan's name has been almost continually in the media for perhaps three years. He has appealed his sentence to the Manitoba Court of Appeal and lost. He went to the Supreme Court because he is one of an increasing group of growers who believe this is all costly anti-democratic nonsense.

This young Canadian is prepared to stand up against the awesome power of the state. Yes, it would be easier for him to just give it all up. Why spend endless hours and days, and now years, fighting the country's flawed politics, trying to change its damaging laws? Why should one individual like David Bryan, despite huge support from other growers, risk all, taking on the state?

10

GROWER FINED $165,000; MONOPOLY SPECULATES LOSES, WITH FARMERS' GRAIN; "WHEAT WALMART ...UNDERCUTS WORLD PRICES"

Ben Hudye spent years and a fortune battling Ottawa for freedom to manage his farm. Why did the monopoly miss the highest farm prices ever? Montana growers astounded at the oppression in Canada's 'administered system'

DO $165,000 IN PENALTIES FOR ONE GROWER HELP BUILD THE WEST?

Ben Hudye received a strange document in his mail in August, '95 - perhaps an unprecedented one for a prairie grain grower. It came from Canada Customs. And it took his breath away. It was a massive fine of $165,000 - in effect, the price Customs/National Revenue was charging him in 'ascertained forfeitures' (fines to be paid later) and 'conveyance' penalties for hauling his grain to the US without export permits. And he was expected to pay that $165,000.

Hudye is a big man physically. And in partnership with his dad Paul and his brother Greg, he farms on a big scale. He lives on their Norquay, Sask., farm. But they have land in the US as well, and in moving back and forth, they constantly spot market opportunities not visible to everyone.

As with every farm family business today, survival is the game. They must respond to every opportunity. Their Hudye Soil Services sells fertilisers and other farm supplies.

And in early '99, Ben was the biggest buyer at the National Bison Association Gold Trophy Show and Sale at Denver, Colorado. He was building their new breeding herd to nearly 100 head. The family also has some elk.

Yes, their farm business reflects an agriculture/food industry in furious change. And Ben has spent years and a small fortune battling Ottawa for the freedom to manage it and to respond to fast-changing markets.

His dispute with Ottawa's grain monopoly went back more than a decade to when he began raising an unregistered wheat variety imported from the US. "We wanted a wheat that took full advantage of north-east Saskatchewan's unique climate," he recalls. "Those US varieties were superior to any we could find in Canada. And they qualified for human consumption over in Minneapolis and would command a much higher price."

But Ottawa's monopoly board put endless obstacles in his way. Its obsession with keeping things large scale and simple to suit its price-pooling export system was a major problem. Registering a new grain variety could take years. And the board decreed that unregistered varieties could only be sold locally as livestock feed. This blocked Hudye from cashing in on beckoning US markets.

Then in 1994 Hudye found some Canadian barley he liked. It only graded feed barley in Canada. But it qualified as malt quality in the US. He needed the money badly so he trucked 126,000 Bu. of it across the border to North Dakota. US beer-maker Anheuser-Busch bought it at a good price.

But he had failed to get an export permit. And Ottawa was outraged at this display of individual initiative, saw it as a challenge to its monopoly. It had already set penalties in mid '94 and Customs officials began stopping US-bound grain trucks or issuing those "ascertained forfeitures."

Then in August, '95, Hudye was hit with that breathtaking fine.

HE DOESN'T INTIMIDATE EASILY! NOT A TEMPER TANTRUM!

As a grower/businessman, Hudye knows one thing for certain - markets are everything. Now he saw that fine as harassment and an attempt at intimidation that was destroying market opportunities

"More and more niche markets are opening up. That's where the future lies for us growers," he said. "Yet the Board is insensitive to niche markets." It was denying growers their future.

Hudye is one grower who doesn't intimidate easily. The battle began to intensify. He accelerated his barley exports, and got on the telephone asking support from other growers. Nearly 300 irate farmers responded, rallying at Boissevain, Man., in early October, '95. They came together in a two-mile-long convoy and headed for the International Peace Gardens border crossing 70 miles south of Brandon.

They didn't hide their intentions. They informed the RCMP and Customs officials that they were peaceful people who wanted to obey the law. But they believed Ottawa had stepped outside the law trying to protect its entrenched bureaucracy. So they had no choice but to protest. They demanded that Ottawa hear their protest.

Three trucks owned by a North Dakota trucking firm and loaded with Hudye's unlicensed barley were seized by Canada Customs for "attempting to leave the country." The US drivers were told penalties of $1358 per truck must be paid before their release. Hudye paid the fines to free the impounded trucks, and Customs allowed three more trucks to go through, promising only to fine him later through the mail.

Ottawa and Customs undoubtedly hoped this attack would force growers to back off. But these border crossings were not temper tantrums. These growers were long-headed business and family men. Their moves were based on bedrock values - not on emotions. They weren't prepared to knuckle under to intimidation.

HUDYE'S SWEEPING CHALLENGE TO OTTAWA JUSTICE

Hudye's response to that $165,000 fine was not to run for cover. Rather, he went on the attack, filing a Statement of Claim in federal court Feb. 2, 1996, against the National Revenue Minister's decisions. Yes, he said, he exported wheat to the US from Sept. 19 to 23, '95, through Customs ports at the Manitoba-US border. And Customs and Excise issued these 'ascertained forfeitures' alleging he was exporting wheat without a valid export license contrary to the Customs Act.

But he claimed the Customs and Wheat Board acts are

too vague to require a grower to show an export license to a Customs officer or to permit such a penalty. And he said his rights under the Charter of Rights were breached because he had been denied information on which the decisions were based. Since he couldn't make proper representations, the Minister's decision should be overturned.

He further claimed the monopoly denied growers their 'mobility rights' and freedom of association as guaranteed by the Canadian Charter of Rights. He also asked the Justice Dept. to declare the Charter had been unlawfully violated and he was entitled to repayment and return of the sums forfeited.

And he claimed interest on that money.

DEPARTMENT OF JUSTICE ASKS FOR TIME

This brash Statement of Claim was a sweeping challenge that went beyond the rights of growers and to the individual rights of every Canadian. And to the very heart of Canada's politics.

Justice Department solicitors decided they had better take this seriously, and asked for more time to file their Statement of Defence. Hudye agreed and Justice lawyers said they would talk to Revenue Canada to develop a formal response.

This Claim by Hudye had predated the Court's stunning Sawatzky ruling which said the Customs Act didn't require growers to produce export permits. That ruling had triggered quick action by Wheat Board Minister Goodale to change the Act. But three years later (Feb. 26, '99) the Hudye Claim still languished, the lawyers seemingly unable to get a decision.

Hudye's solicitor Orest Rosowsky was urging the Federal Court to respond, but the government had failed to file a defence. Hudye accused Ottawa of continuing to prosecute poorer farmers who could not afford to properly defend themselves.

PRAIRIE GROWERS VOTE FOR FREEDOM OF CHOICE

Every scrap of evidence now pointed to one conclusion – Ottawa's grain stranglehold was dedicated to preserving the past, denying the West its future. Any grower with a glimmer of spirit knew he faced obstruction from Ottawa's monopoly on just about any initiative. Hudye had spent years and much money trying to break through it. Hundreds of other growers were also paying dearly for this struggle.

Liberals and politicians of the left and snug-in-the-system bureaucrats didn't want growers noisily questioning that monopoly or criticising its actions. They kept repeating endlessly it was a matter of justice – that if one grower sells his grain for a higher price, it is inevitably at the cost of other growers.

Their simple creed was, "Don't give capitalism a toehold!"

But the mass of farmers were paying dearly for these costly mistakes in their administered industry. And more and more of them were beginning to understand. When Alberta's government asked wheat and barley growers their views on compulsory marketing, they had pleaded for change, with 65% of them voting for freedom of choice.

Even in Saskatchewan with its deep social gospel roots, a government survey found 58% of growers favoured freedom-of-choice. But their cries for change were ignored by Minister Goodale.

Prominent Peace River, Alta., grower and CFFJ member Bill Blake was deeply committed to the struggle. And he observed, "The Wheat Board is a relic from a bygone time. It is coming apart and it has no role in a modern liberalized global trading era."

He predicted, "Dual marketing (freedom of choice) is imminent."

OTTAWA IS "PERSECUTING THE INNOCENT, PROTECTING CRIMINALS"- NCC

President David Somerville of the high profile National Citizen's Coalition was by now furious at Ottawa's continuing attack on growers. His NCC had supported Andy McMechan's family during his incarceration and was helping to pay his legal fees. And National Post columnist Diane Francis had put that aid into a stark perspective, writing that McMechan could have spent six years in jail for refusing to pay $88,793 in fines and compensation.

Now Somerville said, "The Chretien government is persecuting the innocent while protecting criminals. It's no wonder freedom-loving farmers across Western Canada are outraged."

He added, "The wheat board's monopoly and the degradation and persecution of Andy McMechan are right out of the bad old days of the Soviet Empire. The Chretien government should feel a deep sense of shame."

Somerville and his NCC were no newcomers to this freedom struggle. Earlier, NCC had mounted a prairie-wide media campaign that created enough pressure to get McMechan freed from jail and back home before Christmas to share that precious occasion with his wife and children.

"It's frightening," summed up Somerville. "In a society that prides itself as being free and democratic, farmers can be jailed for selling their own grain to the highest bidder. It's not only morally wrong. Its unconstitutional."

Minister Goodale finally yielded to the mounting pressure, held his breath, and called a prairie-wide plebiscite for barley in early '97. He aimed to get growers to stand staunchly behind his monopoly seller's iron grip on wheat and barley sales. But Goodale got a little more than he wanted.

With the plebiscite underway, Somerville mounted a $30,000 media campaign urging growers to vote for freedom on barley sales and against the monopoly. The NCC clearly understood the politics of such a campaign. And it brought heavy artillery into the battle.

It had the martyred McMechan speak at public meetings in Camrose, Taber and Vulcan, Alberta. About 250 people came to each. And its ads focused on one shocking and politically explosive event. They revealed that when Minister Goodale amended the Wheat Board Act with Bill C-72, one section of it required the board to pay the fines and legal costs for any "present or former director, officer or employee" convicted of a criminal act conducted on behalf of the CWB. Growers, of course, would have to pay such costs.

By campaign's end, CFFJ spokesman Ken Dillen reported, "We estimate we have spoken to 500,000 Albertans through public meetings and the media."

BARLEY VOTE SHOWED SINGLE DESK SELLING DOOMED! - MAGUIRE

When the votes were counted, they favored single desk selling. The majority of growers had refused to favour a new dual marketing system which would free them to opt out of the monopoly and sell their own grain. But when Western Grain Growers' Assoc. President Larry Maguire examined those results closely, he found them less decisive. In fact, support for free choice was strong. Yes, 37% of voters said they would be better off without the CWB, even though not a single farm organisation had advocated dismantling it prior to the campaign.

Yes, said Maguire, the plebiscite ended the idea that growers calling for freedom were a lunatic fringe. And to drive home his point, he noted that 20 percent of growers produce about 80 percent of the grain. Polls show that big-acreage growers are most supportive of market choice. So there could be no doubt - most bushels were being delivered unwillingly to the monopoly system.

"SHOW US THE REGULATIONS REQUIRING THOSE EXPORT PERMITS"

Now this long-festering dispute was bursting into the general media. And the issue was simple. More and more growers were seeing farming and food production as a business. They wanted to roll up their sleeves and use every bit of energy and ingenuity and the explosion of technology to grow and market increasing quantities of grain and processed food products into fast-growing world markets.

But as dozens of them were jailed and charged and their cases dragged on in the courts, curious insights began to appear. Their goal was to free themselves to sell grain at world prices. And in the long tradition of farmers being law-abiding, they wanted to comply with the law. But by early '97 they saw more signs that this campaign of terror and humiliation against them, and the resulting court actions and fines and jailings, were a miscarriage of justice. They dared to think that perhaps growers were not the law-breakers after all but rather the victims of a lawless out-of-control government monopoly. Perhaps Ottawa's action denying them the right to market their own grain was illegal.

They had written endlessly to Canada Customs asking reasonable questions. Like, "Show us the regulations that require us to get a permit from the Wheat Board if we want to export our own wheat and barley." And, "If the National Revenue Minister has not written regulations requiring wheat and barley exports to be reported in writing...(how can we determine why) we are required to report (to Customs)?"

But Customs seemed determined to brush them off. Its General Counsel CJ Mainella said he disagreed with the CFFJ interpretation, repeated the tired old rote that an exporter must stop and provide the Customs officer with a copy of the Wheat Board licence. But he didn't offer a copy of the regulations.

The growers refused to be intimidated. "Customs has failed to provide a copy of a regulation issued by the Minister of National Revenue which requires that wheat and barley be reported," they wrote. "As a result, FFJ have concluded growers are not required to report the export of wheat or barley to the Chief Officer of Customs and (growers) now have the same rights in law as all other persons exporting grain to the US."

These growers were also convinced that if they were to be charged at all, it should be under the Wheat Board Act. But Ottawa was charging them under the Customs Act, thus criminalizing their actions even though growers saw their actions as simply protests.

BOARD SPECULATED WITH GROWERS' GRAIN, MISSED "HIGHEST PRICES IN OUR FARMING CAREERS."

Now evidence exploded into the media of another catastrophic error by the monopoly. Barley was piling up in farm bins in the summer of '97 and another crop was ripening in the fields. Prices were desperately low. Growers' fears that the system wasn't working were again proving all too true. They began planning another high-profile challenge – a mass border crossing and a return that same day by a convoy of empty trucks.

They reminded growers in news releases of "..the grain backed up in your own bins at home waiting for the government board to take it and sell it and return some cash to you."

Cause of this new pileup was no mystery to anyone who looked. "Most of that grain could have been delivered earlier," said these growers. "In fact, it should have been sold by the board last fall at between $6 and $8 per Bu. Market prices were at record levels and the CWB missed them. That's why we had record carryovers last year."

What caused this blunder? FFJ growers went right to

the point. "During the highest prices in our farming careers, the board filled the system while it speculated with unsold grain. But it should have been pricing and moving it. The Americans, Australians and Argentineans 'cleaned up and cleaned out' at the high prices.

"And now Canada's board has no sales on the books."

They accused "all the CWB experts" of failing to see the big new crop coming. Yet any farmer "..could have judged his own yields and hedged some in a free market system if Ottawa didn't prevent it."

Now CFFJ pointed to another damning piece of news. The Canadian Pacific Railway reported if all the rail cars unused by the monopoly board the previous summer and fall were lined up on a track they would stretch over 50 miles. If the CNR makes a similar claim, it said, "..that makes 100 miles of empty rail cars doing nothing."

WHY HAD THE BOARD BLUNDERED? WAS IT PART OF A CHEAP FOOD POLICY?

Asked the growers, "Why had the board blundered so badly? Did Ottawa tell it to stop exports to maintain cheap food at farmers' expense? Was it just incompetence because nobody has a stake in the price the grain is sold for? Nobody but you and me, that is.

"The issue is simple," they said. "It is our wheat from the time we buy the seed until the wheat reaches our bins. Where is the Board when we are toiling day and night trying to get the seed into the ground, anxiously looking out for the right rain, trying to stay out of a hailstorm's path?"

And this begged the question, "Why should we take all the risks producing the grain, yet once it is safely in the bin, it is no longer ours?"

These growers asked one final question. "How can we trust someone else with a job that determines the profitability and future of our way of life?" And especially, "..if that person has no farm experience, and has a secure salary, and absolutely no incentive and no mandate to sell at the best price?"

Yes, the pileup's cause was easily explained. It was also a devastating appraisal of Ottawa's monopoly in action.

CFFJ now reminded members of another vital truth. "Growers do very well pricing their own canola and oats and other free market commodities. So shouldn't there be just a simple opt-out from the government's monopoly control of wheat and barley? Because that would free up growers who wanted to sell their own grain."

The issue was crystal clear. Every grower should ask himself, "Can you afford to take $3 for wheat that can be sold for $8 on the open market?"

Grower Bernie Sambrook of Medora, Man., added his own personal view. He could sell his 30 Bu. per acre durum wheat crop for around $7 a Bu. in a free market. But he said, "This fall the CWB will buy only five Bu. per acre at an initial price of $3.83. It will pay the balance next year." Instead of getting over $200 per acre, Sambrook said he would collect $19 per acre and have to wait months for the remaining $140 or so.

Wheat Board Chief Commissioner Lorne Hehn all but confirmed the growers' charges, warning in early August that a projected near-record world wheat crop was causing world prices to fall.

Yes, the evidence was overwhelming. If growers were free to sell their own grain, they could get more money for it.

AT MONTANA MEETING, PRAIRIE GROWERS REVEAL THE BIG CANADIAN PROBLEM

Trade between countries is always a delicate matter. It takes constant communication and reassurance to see that trade is fair and just. And no one recognised this more than these growers in the great Canada-US Western grain belt.

Montana growers had become alarmed back in 1994 that Canada's monopoly was flooding their market with grain priced below market levels. And when farmers Hank Zell and Ron Jensen responded by spearheading a high profile blockade of local Montana elevators, they succeeded in forcing Canada to accept a cap on grain exports there. Their unwavering message was trumpeted out - Canada faced harsh reprisals if it didn't stop shipping in cheap grain.

CFFJ growers saw this as one more example of Canada's failing grain system. Ottawa's bureaucrats were not communicating clearly with neighbouring US farmers or with their politicians. So if the politicians and bureaucrats couldn't do it, growers would have to lead the way themselves.

In early '97, with Canada's grain system still in confusion, growers in both countries were ready to try for more understanding. Those Montana growers Zell and Jensen organised a meeting. And sixteen Canadian growers headed for Shelby, Mon., for serious talks.

Richard Nordstrom was one of them. And this Viking, AB, grower reported later that the meeting was an eye-opener for the Americans. He revealed just how astonished they had been to get the real story of how Canada's administered system worked.

Hank Zell told US growers afterwards, "We were under the mistaken impression....it was western Canadian farmers who were plugging our elevators...But I learned ....the only outfit with the legal authority to sell grain in our market is the state trading enterprise...the CWB and its allies, the wheat pools.

"And while they plug our elevators, we now have irrefutable proof that they are dumping grain into our market at below world prices and that is unacceptable to us Montana farmers."

Nordstrom reported that Ron Jenson had offered further insights to his fellow Montana growers, telling them, "We have learned so much in the past year about the oppression faced by our neighbours to the north - for instance the CWB has the power to jail farmers up there. (In fact)...this government entity operates under Soviet-style secrecy, is not subject to the Freedom of Information Act, is not answerable to the Parliament of Canada, and is not subject to an audit by the auditor general for Canada."

Canadian farmers "..can't even find out how much they pay for in-house fitness facilities and a full-time fitness instruction for Board employees," Jenson added. "They jail farmers for selling to the US, and they prevent N.D. and Montana farmers from selling into the Canadian market."

"WHEAT WAL-MART ATTITUDE LEADS MARKET DOWN, NOT UP"

The growers' freedom fight got further ammunition when President Chuck Merja of the National Association of Wheat Growers in the USA, travelled to Saskatoon in late Oct.'97. He came to talk farm and food policy. And he offered astounding evidence that Canada's monopoly falls far short of its goals.

"..the Wheat Board's 'discounter attitude' makes it hard for farmers on either side of 49th parallel to prosper," he said. In fact, "..this wheat Wal-Mart (approach) ....is probably the biggest impediment to the fair pricing of quality wheat in the world market.

"The board talks a good line about quality," he said. "But it ends up giving that quality away. Canadians have somehow decided that over-filling on protein specs, cleaning wheat without getting a premium for that effort and even giving concessions on base price are the way to do business."

He suggested, "The CWB could be the market leader on the UP side. But it is the market leader on the DOWN side," instead.

He cited examples. "As an engineer, I LIKE NUMBERS. I COMPARED SOME Canadian and US WHEAT PRICES. I ...expected to see some years where Canadian prices were better than US and vice versa. But lo and behold, in not one year was that the case. I compared annual average in-store prices of 1 CWRS Vancouver, adjusted to US dollars, to annual average prices for 1 DNS of the same protein in Portland – I looked at data for the last 25 years. Not once did Canadian prices exceed US prices."

The Wheat Growers' president looked at "standing offer prices in Pacific Rim and Latin American countries to find the best US price." And he found that "the CWB will (undercut it) by $3 to $5 /tonne. Does this put upward or downward pressure on markets?" he asked.

He offered another example. "The CWB sold wheat to Iran a couple of months ago (where there is NO COMPETITION since the US doesn't do business there) for up to $15 a tonne under world prices." And he asked, "Why do that where there is NO COMPETITION? It appears to be force of habit not to maximize returns to farmers, but rather to dump wheat into world markets."

He noted that Canada's Wheat Board Chief Commissioner said, "..he's worried about export subsidies and wants to do away with them. But meanwhile, his outfit makes these price-depressing offers as standard operating procedures."

Merja recalled a Wheat Board attorney saying recently in the Manitoba Court of Appeals, that the Board's only mandate is "..to dispose of the grain in the best interests of the federal government as its agent. It has no obligation to obtain the best price for farmers."

And he protested, "No amount of regulation can substitute for a lack of competition."

Even on the CWB website, he said, you see the discounter attitude. In answering some farmers who collected US prices and compared them to see how the board was doing, it said, "CWB experience trading into the resale elevator markets (in the US) has shown that the 'indication prices' are well above the prices that high quality grain .....can be traded (in volume)into these facilities..."

Merja was appalled at that statement. He told his Saskatoon audience, "I'm here to tell you that I trade wheat at a premium to those 'indicated prices' more times than not." He added, "I challenge the CWB to show any time where they got a premium selling the same quality grain. I don't think they can do it because 'it isn't their mandate.'"

"With this attitude," he said, "it will be hard for farmers on either side of the 49th parallel to prosper. This is why the Montana Grain Growers Assoc. and also the National Assoc. of Wheat Growers have resolutions that read, 'All imports of wheat and barley should come from private party sales. We think individual farmers are better marketers of what they grow than is the wheat Walmart.'"

He added that US farmers would like to see the CWB rethink its "discounter attitude." "PUT THE BOARD AT RISK IN THE MARKET PLACE," he urged. "If it was truly at risk and had to worry about replacement cost of sales, it would rethink its discounter attitude or it would have trouble procuring product."

Merje also rejected attacks on US food subsidy programs. "The European Union...has doubled wheat production and tripled exports in the last 20 years," he said. Stretch out the time a little more, and you see they have gone from a net wheat importer to a net exporter - a production swing of roughly 140% of Canada's total annual production. And they did it not by comparative advantage, but with major intervention that goes on even today at a level roughly 10 times that of the US

Merja said, "I will take exception to the Wheat Board Commissioner's US subsidy chart - I wish he had shown it all the way out to 2002, when it goes to zero. And I might add that the US hasn't used the Export Enhancement Program since July, 1995 (even though it can be GATT legal)."

He called for further improvements to the world trading system, "to allow food and other products to flow from areas of surplus to areas of need."

Two statistics made his point. "First the world has used more wheat than it raised in 7 of the last 10 years. And the world has tripled food production in the last 30 years."

He added that by most measures we will need to triple it again in the next 30 to 40 years, on less land mass than we currently use and in environmentally sound ways. Surplus and deficit areas are certain in that scenario. And unless we have good rules, we will see trouble.

11

THAT 'IMPOSSIBLE VALUE-ADDED DREAM' IS HERE, BUT POLITICS CHASES THE KIDS AWAY

These growers have gone organic, produce an array of delicacies which are in demand across Canada and beyond. Their 'Swedish Soup Mix with Herbs' is a best seller. This 'value-added' is a recipe for prairie growth. But why are the kids leaving the farms and the West?

SWING TO VALUE-ADDED

You'll find Carol and John Husband just about any Saturday in summer caught up in the bustling activity in their big and ageless Market Barn. Customers are flocking in to plan their meals for the week ahead. They are feasting their eyes on the fresh green beans and peas and beets and carrots grown by the Husbands and by neighbouring growers. And they are selecting the foods they want including Carol's now-famous Swedish Soup Mix with Herbs, and six other mixes.

Beyond the bustle of that barn is an enterprise reflecting a food industry in breathtaking change. Those 1760 acres of land near Wawota in south-eastern Saskatchewan go deep into prairie history. The buildings are on a farm homesteaded by John Husband's grandfather in 1900. Carol's family settled in 1883 on a farmstead 60 miles north.

Respect for that century of building by their ancestors is etched into the very souls of Carol and John today. Nostalgia could become a way of life. But when this couple can find a few minutes to chat together, they aren't reminiscing. They are focused on a beckoning challenge.

Yes, in today's fast-moving world, any farmer/food producer who wants to serve a new generation of consumers must have a vision for the future. And back in 1988, Carol and John began to see a dramatic shift in society. A new generation of consumers was focusing on healthy living. This spelled 'OPPORTUNITY!' written large for growers. Organic farming in which crops are grown largely without the use of agricultural chemicals, met these new needs. And it offered growers a way to add value to their crops right on their own farms.

"Don't grow ordinary crops. Grow extra-value ones," was the message. And the Husbands responded. All their land is now 'Certified Organic.'

Then these venturing growers got lucky again. They got a bag of Swedish Brown beans. And, too-good-to-be-true, these descended from seed stock brought to Saskatchewan in the 1880's by Swedish pioneers - Carol's great-grandmother among them.

John set out to grow them, and in four years, he had enough to seed a market crop. As it turned out, he and Carol couldn't have made a better decision. Demand for organic foods has become almost a craze. It isn't based on any startling new research evidence. No, this industry has been built in response to consumer demand and without the solicitous advice of government experts and without the supposed benefit of government money grants. Demand for their foods may be expanding exponentially. Price premiums can be high.

A UNIQUE AND IRRESISTIBLE FLAVOUR

A kitchen holds no mysteries for Carol. And she understands perfectly the fine art of entertaining. Chuckles John, "I grow, Carol cooks, and we all eat."

As it turned out, those Swedish Brown beans cooked up with a unique and irresistible flavour. Why couldn't they be packaged with herbs and spices to make highly marketable soups? Carol devised mixes rich with these fresh herbs.

"Here is something we can really sell," thought the Husbands. So they went one step further. The big old stone barn built by John's grandfather in 1925 was still sound and in good repair. It could be an ideal premise for direct-selling specialty foods to consumers. They made needed renovations, then fastened on a huge sign, **"The Market Barn,"** proclaiming their vital message to passers-by on the highway out front.

They began processing that food right there on the farm. The first was their Swedish Soup Mix with Herbs featuring their uniquely flavoured brown beans. Others followed. They blend those Swedish Browns with other beans including Ireland Creek Annie and Pinto. They add a small pack of tangy ground herbs and spices they also grow. And they package them under their 'Husband's Foods' brand name, ready for the consumer.

Growing and marketing these organic foods was fast becoming their obsession. And it was transforming their lives. Now, from June to September, they are caught up in that endless marketing challenge. And with two dozen friends and neighbours joining them, they are selling an endless variety of vegetables and fruits and preserves, and prepared foods from that 'Market Barn.'

But these direct sales to buyers who come right to their farm is only a small part of their business. The Husbands had decided, "Lets go right to the consumer."

And they haven't looked back. More than half their land is now growing heritage and specialty crops little known or grown elsewhere in Canada or beyond. And these are catching on with homemakers, retailers and chefs across the country.

In this fast-changing world, markets for bulk grains are growing in the US and Europe and now in Japan. And John and Carol are selling aggressively into them. Most of their bulk grain goes out from their farm in big semi trucks on its way across Canada and to Europe, or heading south to the US.

They are finding this organic niche makes farming viable on their rich farmland. And they are not alone. Increasing numbers of growers are responding to those new opportunities.

"Focus on the ultimate consumer," they say. "By-pass bureaucratic middlemen. Go value-added!"

AVOID WHEAT, BARLEY, BECAUSE OF OTTAWA'S OBSTACLES

Yes, the Husbands are value-adders to the crops they grow. But for an unbelievable reason, they try to avoid the two crops which are synonymous with the very development of the prairie breadbasket. Despite good market demand for wheat and barley, and despite their importance to crop rotation in organic farming, Ottawa's sales monopoly and its backward policies throw too many obstacles in the way.

The Husbands were in the purebred Hereford cattle business for 22 years, selling breeding stock all over the world, before they shifted to wheat and other crops. They assumed they could sell those crops freely, as they had their cattle. One early episode with the monopoly opened their eyes in astonishment.

They had contracted their organic wheat crop to an organic miller in Quebec, writing a legal business contract. Then, the miller called. He was almost out of wheat. He needed wheat delivered by Monday.

Here's what happened next. The monopoly board prohibited them from selling their wheat to Quebec without first going through a 'buy-back' from the monopoly. In fact, it had turned out that Ottawa's monopoly was seizing ownership of their wheat at the time they harvested it.

"We called the local elevator to ask the buy-back price," Carol recalls. "The agent said he would get a price quote from the Board. He soon called back, 'We couldn't have the buy-back at any price. The Wheat Board would NOT allow it. Period.'

"That left us dazed. If we didn't deliver, the miller could sue us for breach of contract. If we did, the CWB would fine us for selling without doing the buy-back.

"What would we do? We decided we'd better sell the wheat so we could at least pay any fines levied on us. We arranged for the transport. Then the Board called back. It had reconsidered. It would allow the buy-back."

But if the monopoly hadn't changed its mind, what would the Husbands' liability have been for a defaulted contract, they wondered?

Carol immediately contacted the board "..to ask about our legal rights when we contract. Its legal counsel responded on Jan 12, 1995, 'The Board has discretion not to grant any license at all. But if it does decide to grant a license, it sets the terms/conditions.'"

A shocked Carol asked, "How can we contract to buyers if we are prevented from selling the grain. Only the CWB decides. No arbitration board or ombudsman is in place. The Board is immune from the Freedom of Information Act."

In fact, the high buy-back price often prevents organic producers making the sale. She called it, "A frightening lack of accountability."

SHE TELLS SENATORS, VALUE ADDED MAKES SENSE, PLEADS FOR FREEDOM

When the Senate held hearings into possible changes to Ottawa's oppressive monopoly in 1998, Carol was one of the many growers who came out to address the senators. And she told them a remarkable story. Value-added farming makes business sense, she said. From a mere handful of organic farms a decade ago, a 1997 survey found 230 such farms in Saskatchewan and 110 in Alberta.

"All without government central planning and without growers begging for tax money," she emphasised.

She went on to tell how that monopoly board so often stands in the way of progress, battling any move by growers to specialise and move into higher paying niche markets. In its obsession with averages, this "great leveller" seizes ownership of almost every bushel of wheat and barley prairie growers harvest for sale.

She described how it obstructs these new value-added farms. In the politics-strangled and crisis-ridden prairie farm industry, she observed that politicians and news headlines seem to always get it wrong. They never fail to focus on short-term problems and disputes, which continually flash onto every TV screen in the country. But the politicians too often ignore opportunities and solutions.

Yes, countless politicians and bureaucrats fight to preserve one of their last bastions of power and control - the huge prairie grain industry. And the west itself.

"Protect farmers from the evil market place," has been their war cry for decades. And the justification for their uncounted cushy jobs.

ORGANIC GROWERS BEGIN TO REQUEST EXEMPTIONS

With Ottawa's politicians so often standing in their way, the organic farmers began to ask for exemptions. And then, in one hopeful step, the Wheat Board set up a Value-Added Enhancement Study Committee which proclaimed it wanted "producer input."

A group of 67 grass-roots organic farmers - the Organic Special Products Group - responded expressing strong opposition to Ottawa's monopoly marketing of organic grain and sending copies of their statement to Minister Ralph

Goodale and to the monopoly board.

Goodale replied that a study was in the works. And he promised their letter would go to the monopoly board. Board Chief Lorne Hehn wrote that the board's committee would contact all segments of the value-added industry.

Meanwhile growers and the industry came together on the national level jointly setting up a Canadian Organic Advisory Board (COAB.) But the monopoly's new Value-Added Enhancement Study Committee stated that this new grower/industry Organic Advisory Board favoured ".. the CWB's role as single-desk seller." It added, "..this role could be expanded to include more CWB marketing of organic products."

Here was an astonishing piece of news. The Organic Advisory Board was supposedly a non-partisan national body representing growers and industry. It had been set up to deal solely with organic industry standards. But this statement was politically partisan.

Carol Husband set out to identify the origin of this report attributed to the Advisory Board. She found that University of Saskatchewan economist Dr. Richard Gray had compiled the organic section of the Value Added Study. But ominously, he failed to include the views of the 67 grass-roots organic farmers.

She drove home her point. "No wonder the average farmer has lost faith in the board, in governments and in many of the institutions that presume to speak for agriculture. Growing numbers of farmers remain steadfast in opposition to the wheat board and its political masters. And that won't change until treatment of growers changes."

She exploded in frustration, "The farm community deserves better."

GROWERS FIGHT BACK

Organic growers including the Husbands and hundreds of others through the West have made massive investments in building this new value-added industry which promises to bring their farms back to profitability, creating huge returns for the West and for endless farm communities, and creating myriad jobs in growing, processing, marketing and beyond. But these growers know it won't be easy, for they face the massive wheat board bureaucracy and its consuming political interests.

John Husband leaves no doubt - growers simply want to be freed up to market their own grains. But bureaucrats and politicians insist the board has no choice – the law compels it to charge them the "buy-back" if they want to market their own grain.

Husband's simple response is, "We don't want to sell to the wheat board, we want to sell to our customers. The board is an impediment to us."

And now a wheat board internal memo that recently came public has shone a whole new light on the board's story. That memo deals with a section of farming country in lower British Columbia adjacent to Alberta called the Creston/Wynndel area which until recently was part of the "Designated Area," where the Board had total control over Board grains.

That internal memo (released by the CWB as part of its legal defense in one of its many court cases,) let the cat out of the bag. It revealed that, yes, the board did give growers there the freedom to export their grain to the USA without the buyback. And that shed a whole new light on the burning freedom issue. It left no doubt – the Wheat Board Act does not prevent the monopoly from giving growers no-cost export licenses so they can export without a buyback.

In the eyes of hundreds of prairie organic growers, this is final proof – the board can free up any growers in the Designated Area to sell their own grain if it chooses. So it is not the law that denies them a no-cost export permit - it must be simply Ottawa's politicians who are standing in the way.

That means one thing is certain. Those growers will continue to press for the freedom to manage their own farms. For that freedom is vital if they are to save their own farms, their communities, their industry, and perhaps the West as well.

OPPORTUNITIES NEVER BRIGHTER – BUT THE KIDS ARE LEAVING

In these times of change and opportunity, the experience of John and Carol Husband leave no doubt - a simple, logical, but for too long impossible dream is suddenly within reach. Grow an increasingly wide range of crops on fertile prairie farm land, process them right on the farm, or in the local communities, and market those products directly to the consumer not only in local markets, but in world markets too. What could be more logical? A younger generation of prairie growers should be rubbing its hands in anticipation

But as these growers know to their cost, government interference is front and centre in blocking off that beckoning world. No wonder the kids are attracted to new growth industries that offer them opportunity and independence and wealth. And too many of them are fleeing Saskatchewan, and often the prairies, heading for those greener pastures. They are taking their skills and their wealth-producing abilities with them, often leaving Canada for the U.S.

MARKET PLACE THREATENS POLITICAL ELITES

One wise observer explained it simply. "The dynamic market place erodes the ability of political elites to enforce collective decisions."

Yes, monopoly Wheat Board politicians and bureaucrats comprise a 'political elite.' And they are busy imposing bureaucratic decisions on farmers and denying them free access to the market place.

Yet the record of ruling political elites is a sad one. The market place is the only source of freedom for most of us in this society. And the Husbands and thousands of other growers know this to their horrendous cost. But Ottawa's Liberals seem unable to grasp the point.

Look closely and you'll see it. Feeding the hungry may be the world's greatest challenge. Yet Ottawa's Wheat Board policies have devastated growers and hurt one of the world's most fertile breadbaskets. That's why Canada's prairie agriculture is in such desperate trouble.

12

IS MONOPOLY RIFE WITH ARROGANCE, CONFLICT OF INTEREST, FASCISM?

Fresh insights offered a devastating picture - poli-ticians and bureaucrats were too often the bosses, while growers paid the bills and paid the price.

A NEW AND DISTURBING INSIGHT INTO THE MONOPOLY'S STORY

Most Westerners applaud these days as old Communist states abandon their failed monopolies and free up their people to respond to market forces. Imitation is the sincerest form of flattery. And in our western culture, that free market has been the key to the most precious prize of all - personal freedom.

Free markets have enabled Western societies to boot out bureaucrats, replace them with citizens who must provide service to the public or lose their jobs. And the ingenuity and energy and boldness and responsibility of free people working in a free market system have created wealth and built our culture and our society. Nations wanting to free their people to escape poverty and despair have no choice but to "imitate" our Western successes.

Yes, the days when government bureaucrats can bark out orders to the public should be long gone. But some surprising behind-the-scenes events that have accidentally come to light offer new insights into the wheat board story and perhaps explode that idea. They certainly raise the question, Does Ottawa's Liberal government really understand this freedom issue? Or do Canadians?

NEW PANEL TO SEEK GRAIN MARKETING FLAWS

Wheat Board Minister Goodale decided in 1995 he had

better ask growers about any flaws they saw in the workings of Canada's grain monopoly. He set up a Western Grain Marketing Panel, naming its members carefully. And he assigned it the job of looking into this politically-charged issue.

As Goodale's panel was getting its meetings underway, a curious thing happened. Copies of memos dealing with upcoming Panel meetings began circulating furiously on the widespread fax network of Canadian Farmers For Justice growers. No-one knew just how these documents had come into the growers' hands or where they had originated. But they became a matter of feverish discussion.

The three memos were on Wheat Board letterhead. And they offered a surprising glimpse into behind-the-scenes actions by Canada's biggest monopoly which holds enormous power over every farmer. In fact, they outlined what seemed to be a covert Board strategy to influence the Marketing Panel's meetings. Growers who read them were infuriated, asked,"Is something really going on?"

THAT FIRST MEMO

The first memo, dated Jan 4, '96, was headed, "Inter-Office Correspondence" coming from "The Canadian Wheat Board." It was signed by 'Brian White' who was identified as Director of the CWB's Market Analysis Department, and was titled "Proposal for In-Camera Meetings Between Canadian Wheat Board (CWB) Staff and Saskatchewan Wheat Pool (SWP) and Alberta Wheat Pool (AWP) directors and delegates on CWB Marketing."

It was addressed to 'Glen McGlaughlin, John Petruic' (who were respectively of the Saskatchewan and Alberta Pools.)

This confidential memo opened a surprising can of worms. It said, "CWB staff will be travelling to various locales in Alberta and Saskatchewan this month to attend the Western Grain Marketing Panel (WGMP) town-hall meetings (at the WGMP's request) as resource people."

Then came the alarming proposition: "..the CWB is offering.....to hold in-camera meetings with however many SWP and AWP district directors/delegates can be available in each WGMP meeting date."

The next sentence brought a howl of disbelief from CFFJ recipients. "Purpose of these in-camera meetings," it read, "would be for the CWB staff member to give Pool directors/

delegates a private briefing on the CWB marketing system and how it benefits farmers, using specific and confidential CWB sales and marketing information to illustrate this."

And the memo said this would be " .followed by a **frank and open discussion** on CWB marketing and other issues."

More than one CFFJ grower who picked these off the fax and read them raised one overriding question: Just how frank and open would that "frank and open discussion on CWB marketing and other issues," be? Was the Wheat Board really feeding confidential information to favoured growers? That would mean mean some growers had more information than others. And their information would be slanted.

As background, White seemed to have stated that CWB staff held six small in-camera district meetings with Manitoba Pool Elevators' district directors and delegates in December, prior to the Marketing Panel town-hall meetings, at the request of Manitoba Pool and its senior management. These meetings allowed key MPE people to hear the board's pitch on the merits of it being the sole marketer of wheat and barley.

Farmers For Justice growers were understandably livid when the memo went on that this presentation was "..supported by specific concrete (and highly confidential – hence our stipulation that the meetings be in-camera) sales evidence drawn from some of the key sales we have made this crop year." And that Manitoba Pool felt, "Its delegates would subsequently be somewhat better-equipped to discuss CWB marketing and CWB marketing issues with their district councils........"

THE SECOND MEMO

The second memo dated the following day was directed to Saskatchewan and Alberta. It was an "Office Memorandum" on the "CWB Proposal for In-Camera Meetings with SWP/AWP District Directors and Delegates." Again it carried the 'Brian White' signature and copies were directed to: "Board, Measner, Oleson, Redmond, Spafford, Bacon, Brooks, Roehle, Geddes, Harris, Macdonald, Poole, Welsensel."

In that memo, 'White' reported he and Bob Roehle (Wheat Board communictions chief) had talked to McGlaughlin and Petruic, "..to propose that the CWB hold in-camera meetings with SWP and AWP district directors and delegates....just prior to the (Marketing Panel) town-hall meetings on the dates of those same meetings and in the same locales....

"They were both very interested and asked for a description of our proposal in writing that they could discuss with their presidents today. I have faxed (this) to both of them...They are to get back to us today on this, given that the WGMP meetings start next week."

THE MOOD CHANGES

A third memo, dated Jan. 8, titled "SWP and AWP responses to CWB Proposal for in-Camera Meetings," revealed a note of caution was creeping in. It reported that Glen McGlaughlin said SaskPool "..was interested in seeing such meetings occur." And a memo went to its Board of Directors and all district representatives to alert them to this offer by the CWB. "The district representatives are directed to follow up with me directly if they want to set up such an in-camera meeting in their district on the date and at the location of the WGMP town-hall meeting," wrote White.

But Alberta farmers smelled trouble in these curious events. Alberta Wheat Pool's John Petruic was informed his "..delegate membership is divided on...support for the CWB marketing system, (so) there would be a problem in their offering in-camera meetings with the CWB only to selected AWP delegates (those within striking distance of a WGMP town-hall meeting)..."

Reason for the concern was simple. "..those that did not....meet in-camera with the CWB and who were anti-CWB would ask why this hadn't been offered to all AWP delegates..."

In fact, those left out "..would raise a stink about it with their representatives on the AWP Board of Directors." The Board apparently was informed "..such a proposal by the CWB for in-camera meetings would normally have (to be)discussed and approved by the AWP Board of Directors." But the Board wasn't meeting for another three weeks, so this was impossible.

GROWERS ANGRY ABOUT SECRETIVE MEMORANDA

Growers Mark and Ralph Melle of Minton, Sask. were

among those at the centre of the uproar triggered by these memos. And they wrote a "news release/letter-to-the-editor," that drew back the curtain of secrecy on these astonishing events.

They revealed that "..about 300 farmers, men and women, attended the Western Grain Marketing Panel meeting at Weyburn to express their thoughts." A person from the Winnipeg Grain Exchange was also there and one from the Canada Grain Commission. Two Canadian Wheat Board officials, Mr. Eron Gross and Mr. Brian White, were there and they "..circulated through the workshop part of the meeting answering any questions and concerns the farmers might have."

The Melles brothers wrote that Gross was questioned "..as to the private meetings held with Pool directors and delegates" that day. And he answered that they had been cancelled when, "..hours prior to the (Marketing Panel) meetings the CWB had decided not to have those in-camera meetings with the Pool directors and delegates before these last two WGMP meetings."

The Melles asked the key question. "Could this mean that the underhanded information-fixing of meetings could leave a bad taste in the public's mouth?"

They noted that Brian White's name was on the CWB in-office correspondence that set up the private meetings with the Pool directors and delegates in Alberta and Saskatchewan. And their news release then offered another fascinating insight. It reported that most farmers at the Weyburn meeting said "..major change was needed in policy and structure if the CWB was to continue as a viable choice."

It added, "..about 50% of the farmers at the meeting wanted dual Marketing for wheat and Barley."

"IF YOU DON'T LIKE OUR SELLING SYSTEM, GO TO THE U.S.!"

The Melles news release reported another shocking event which shed more light onto these strange actions of Ottawa's grain monopoly. In talking with a table of Minton area farmers, the Wheat Board's White was asked a probing question. "Since the Board's final payment seemed short of expectations, what happened to the rest of the money?"

This brash question seemed to lack a proper respect for the ruling board's officials, and White apparently lost his cool. Several of the growers quoted him later as growling, "If you people don't like the system we have in Canada, then you can move to the United States."

Calls of shame rose from the crowd each time White's statement was repeated at the podium. And the growers put that astonishing remark into a stark perspective in their news release.

"We believe Mr. White is paid directly out of farmers' funds by the CWB," they wrote. "So would an apology be in order? Is this condescending attitude the order of the day at our CWB Head Office? Perhaps if farmers have a choice, the CWB could become business partners with the farmers, rather than our masters."

Yes, these were shocking events. Did they reveal a more honest picture of that powerful Ottawa monopoly than the public had previously known? This evidence suggested that its staff, paid by prairie growers, had set up secret meetings. And they had invited carefully selected farmers who favoured its monopoly selling system while excluding growers who might prefer to sell their own grain. Then secret information was presented.

AN OMINOUS QUESTION - CAN MONOPOLY FAVOUR SOME GROWERS?

These secret behind-closed-doors activities raised an ominous question in the minds of Mark and Ralph Melles. Why would the CWB hold these manipulative meetings pandering to the views of some growers and undermining those with different views?

"Could such a manipulation of our political decision-making process, be condoned? When every farmer pays the costs of running the monopoly, how could those who would prefer to break free and sell their own grain, be excluded from these meetings? How could information that is vital to managing their own farms and shaping their industry, be denied them?

"And is it tolerable that growers who pay all the costs of Ottawa's monopoly system, are told by a paid employee, 'If you don't like the grain selling system we have in Canada, then go to the United States.'"

In fact, these events underlined one other glaring truth. Alberta's growers aren't easy to indoctrinate and they ask tough questions at meetings. And Saskatchewan growers were quickly learning how to recognise self-serving bureaucrats.

Yes, most farmers now wanted change in board policy and structure. About half of them wanted dual marketing for wheat and barley which would give them freedom of choice. The board's goal of shifting growers' views back to solid support for the monopoly was simply impossible to achieve.

"IS THE MONOPOLY A FASCIST MODEL? YES, SAYS THE ENCYCLOPAEDIA"

Bill Blake is a 1750-acre Peace River, Alta., grower who brings a broad perspective to his view of our grain selling system. A retired Canadian Airlines Captain, he has a lively enquiring mind. And he has travelled the world gaining remarkable insights into how our world works. He believes he has a clear understanding of this monopoly board which seizes his wheat and barley each year when he harvests it.

In a letter-to-the-editor he titled, "Under the Boot," in April, '96, he explained precisely why he calls the Board monopoly a "Fascist Model."

"Monopoly...supporters desperately want to avoid a discussion of what the Board does to individual liberty and to freedoms of prairie people," he wrote. And he asked, "What is the Wheat Board? A co-op?"

He answered his own question, "No! A co-op by definition is voluntary, not compulsory.

"Is it socialism? It can't be. The means of production here aren't government-owned but in private hands.

"See if this description fits," he wrote. "The means of production are in private hands though under tight government control.

"That's what the World Book Encyclopaedia has to say about Fascism. Under the Wheat Board Act, elevators, railways, mills and farms are privately owned but under tight government control. It would appear the Wheat Board's monopoly (established in 1943) is a Fascist model. Webster's definition of Fascism is '..economic and social regimentation and forcible suppression of opposition.' If the shoe fits..."

Such was the desperation of the growers impacted by the Board's actions they were driven to compare the monopoly to similar programs under fascist regimes in the past.

"Webster calls Fascism, 'a political philosophy that exalts the state above the individual,'" Blake continued.

"Oppression, subservience of each citizen to the state and the loss of individual liberty are the price of the Wheat Board model no matter how sunny a mask they try to put on it," said Blake. "The police raids on farmers' homes, criminal charges and arbitrary fines have let the stark face of reality show through. **It is fear that backs it all up.**

"Some Wheat Board monopoly supporters may not even realise they are supporting a Neo-Fascist system, but they are. They are really saying to farmers, 'If you dare to disagree with me, I will support the use of all the power of the State to forcibly drag you in.'

"Hopefully those who want to keep their region under the boot of the Wheat Board monopoly will no longer be followed. We want a truly free and prosperous country. **State control has been tried and thrown out virtually everywhere else except here in the 'designated area' Western Canada. Its time we end** the experience."

Blake concluded, "What most people want is the security of economic growth, opportunity, jobs and a free society."

Who would disagree with him?

IS PRAIRIE GRAIN MARKETING RIFE WITH CONFLICT OF INTEREST?

Saskatchewan grower Carol Husband had always said farmers must regain the right to sell their own wheat and barley. And since marketing prairie wheat is an exercise in politics rather than business, she wanted to know what forces and people might impact on Ottawa's determination to hold tight to its wheat monopoly policy. She has looked hard at some of the decision-makers who influence it. She tried to follow the money.

Everyone knows the facts of farm life, she explains. The Wheat Board monopoly is tightly controlled by Ottawa politicians. They take legal ownership of wheat and barley grown on prairie farms. They usually ship the grain east. Grain has traditionally gone through the Great Lakes and the Atlantic Seaway, even if the farmers who grew it would have preferred to ship it south or ship it west. Or even if those growers would have preferred to process it right at home to gain the benefits of value-added and help build the prairie economy.

On reading Canadian author/historian Peter Newman's book, "The Canadian Establishment, Volume 1," Husband got a blinding insight into a powerful Eastern elite with close connections to Ottawa's politicians. And she asked, Could any of this affect wheat marketing?

In contemplating this power elite, Husband said one would have to ask a serious question. "Who in our monopoly cares about farmers who want to sell their own grain or to process it and add value in the west - keeping the money here?"

AN OBSCENE DISCOVERY - BOARD SEVERANCE PACKAGE $250,000!

Ted Cawkwell is a past president of the Western Barley Growers Assoc. More recently he was president of the Prairie Centre - a private Regina-based unit set up to offer growers more information and a better understanding of grain marketing issues. On occasion, it exerts political pressure for legislation to allow farmers to grow and market their crops more profitably.

Cawkwell farms near Nutt Mountain, Sask. In late '95, during his term as its president, that Prairie Centre dug out some information which proved to be another devastating signal. It showed the monopoly board was failing badly in its most important challenge - the need to keep prairie growers and their organisations on side and in full support of its efforts.

Here is what happened. Times were tough on the farm. Growers were struggling to survive. Many were going under. But despite the monopoly Board's stonewalling, the Prairie Centre found that Wheat Board Commissioners were able to collect severance packages running to over $250,000.

That severance money came directly out of growers' pockets. Many of them saw this as an outrageous, even obscene, bit of news. As well as an astonishing insight into the flawed grain marketing system.

Cawkwell showed the evidence that US growers were getting massively higher returns than the wheat board could pull in, simply by selling their grain on open world markets. And he never hesitated to venture onto this dangerous political ground. He put out a news release from the Prairie Centre revealing that remarkable sum. He asked hard questions about farmers' hard-earned money.

In fact, he called the board the most secretive government agency in the country outside of Canada's spy agencies, said it even refuses to answer simple questions like salary levels and pension benefits available to commissioners and senior bureaucrats.

"Such information is available from virtually any government agency, whether it be provincial, municipal or federal," said Cawkwell. "Yet the CWB refuses to provide answers."

And legislatively, it does not answer to anyone but the government.

RUSS LARSON SAYS MONOPOLY MARKETING SHOWS GROSS INEFFICIENCY!

Russ Larson is an Outlook, Sask., grower who was an early member of Farmers for Justice and then became a founder and president of its spinoff, Canadian Farm Enterprise Network. He is a skillful writer and has sent out dozens of news releases on these grower activities. He went to the guts of the issue in July, '97, with perhaps the best column of all.

"For 54 years Western Canadian farmers have had their grain confiscated by the federal government...been paid less than their American colleagues..(with)..the devastating result that millions upon millions of dollars have been siphoned by mostly Liberal governments."

Larson looked back over too many years of political deviousness and bureaucratic bungling. And he wrote, "For 54 years we have seen incompetence in the marketing of grain...(the board has been)..giving protein away and supplying premium grades for low quality grain contracts."

He went on, "..this winter we have seen how our transportation is fouled up by the CWB which has ultimate control of allocation of elevator space, cars and ships. With prices dropping in the new crop year we can no longer afford Ralph Goodale's entrenched system."

Larson offered convincing evidence that the CWB shows another characteristic of central planning - gross inefficiency. In the first four months of '97, up to 50 ships lay in BC harbours waiting to be loaded. That pile-up cost growers millions in demurrage fees. Yet the terminals were filled to 80% capacity - enough to load 20 ships.

Why weren't those ships loaded? Larson's answer was simple - the CWB and its central planners had shipped the wrong grain to port. Then they blamed the railroads.

"Socialism and central planning destroyed the potential of many European and Asian economies," he noted. "Is that now happening here in Canada?"

And could growers really win their struggle for freedom? In an April, '97, news release, Larson said this farmers' group has gone from 'a small band of renegades' (in the words of its enemies) to "a force to be reckoned with." He urged all members "..who have worked so hard to get us this far, pat yourselves on the back."

GROWERS WANT GRAIN CHEQUES, NOT GOVERNMENT CHEQUES - SAMBROOK

Weeks later, Larson told of one more grower's bitter and costly experience. "Bernie Sambrook is a young farmer from Medora, Man. And he says, 'Tens, even hundreds of thousands of dollars are being withheld from each western farmer by the CWB Act. Yet if we had a free wheat market I could sell my entire 40 Bu. per acre durum crop for $7 per Bu. or hard red spring for $5.

"'Because of the CWB buying monopoly over me which works with restrictive quotas and only pays us a down payment, all I'll be able to sell this fall is about 5 Bu. of durum for $3.83 or wheat at $2.22. Instead of grain revenue of over $200 per acre, all I can get is $11.'"

Sambrook concluded, "Farmers don't want government cheques, they want grain cheques."

Grower John Husband of Wawota, Sask., added, "Last summer the CWB withdrew from the market when prices were at their highest. This fouled up shipping during the winter and now it is reneging on its contracts with farmers, forcing them to carry inventory into the new crop year when it will be sold for cut-rate prices. It is time to stop this madness."

CENTRAL PLANNING CAN'T EXIST IN MODERN HIGH-TECH ECONOMY – EISLER

"The idea of central planning was the foundation of

communism," wrote Senior Maclean's Magazine writer, Dale Eisler, in the April 17, '97, Saskatoon Star-Phoenix. But he said, "It simply cannot exist in a high-technology, modern economy that is constantly changing."

Much of the world has now rejected Marxist-Leninist solutions to economic problems.

In fact, said Eisler, Prof. Francis Fukuyama of George Mason U., Washington, DC, wrote that socialism failed for a simple reason: "A modern economy requires a decentralised and open market to operate efficiently. And that is the very opposite of central planning."

CFFJ growers probed more deeply and added, "What escapes Eisler is that in western Canada we have the last bastion of discredited socialist central planning, the CWB."

They concluded, "If a Canadian farmer truly owned his grain and could sell it to the highest bidder he would get far more money than he gets now when his wheat and barley is confiscated by Ottawa."

13

"STALINIST GRIP DENIES GROWERS THEIR RIGHTS, MOCKS FREEDOM"

Alex McWilliams was out of pocket $50,000 on one durum crop, and such losses go on year after year. Senate ignores his freedom cry. Winnipeg's decline as world grain centre and as a city.

"STALINIST GRIP DENIES GROWERS THEIR RIGHTS, MOCKS FREEDOM"

Like just about every prairie farm boy a generation or two ago, Alex McWilliams had it drilled into his head that capitalism was bad, the market place was inevitably rigged and private grain company people couldn't be trusted. He was taught the farmer's only hope was to put honest politicians in charge of the vast and priceless grain business.

Then those politicians could appoint their own people as the honest bureaucrats to do what was right for growers and return to them a fair price for their wheat and barley. No wonder McWilliams, and tens of thousands like him, were ardent government wheat board supporters from the start.

But this Pilot Mound, Manitoba, grower's patience has long been exhausted. Too often, that monopoly has failed him and the industry itself, at enormous financial cost. To say nothing of the damage done to the West and to Canada's nationhood.

By early 1998, Ottawa was responding hesitantly to this litany of failures and to growers' rising discontent. A Senate committee set up hearings across the west into a proposed Bill C-4 to amend the Wheat Board Act. McWilliams came to the hearings in Winnipeg well prepared.

And he described a parade of "marketing problems" that had been devastating his farm and those of other growers and the industry.

$50,000 OUT OF POCKET ON ONE DURUM CROP

He told the senators how he grew 18,000 bushels of durum on 600 acres in 1992. But the board's quota was only 5 Bus. per acre. By January the monopoly had taken only 3000 bus. He was told there would be no further quotas that crop year. Yet the monopoly's iron rules prevented him selling the rest to beckoning US markets.

His bins remained almost full and when he and his son heard durum was moving into the US, "...we took a sample to the elevator at Clyde, ND. It weighed 59 1/2 lbs per Bu. and graded 3 CW in Canada. The US buyer said it would grade No. 1 and he would take all we had.

"We learned that a Wheat Board export permit was required, and we would have to go through the buy-back process. The US price for durum was $5.35 (Cdn.). The buy-back would cost us $5.45 and we would have to post it up front. This meant borrowing from the bank and repaying it later when we sold the grain.

"Our banker said, 'No way!' So we were beat.

"Up to then, we realised about $2.20 per Bu., on the 5-Bu. quota or $6,000. You can't farm on $11 an acre - we needed a cash advance! In that winter of 1993, we made many phone calls to the Wheat Board Winnipeg office, asking for a rule change so we could market our grain in the US.

"But Wheat Board people didn't seem to realise they were responsible to market our grain or give us the right to market it ourselves. The monopoly's rules cost us $50,000 on that one crop. We are out of pocket that much from this experience."

No wonder he observed, "We lost any confidence we had for them. We later learned that other growers also lost heavily from the buy-back."

The monopoly was costing growers, the West and the country billions of dollars and adding fuel to western alienation.

BURNING CROPS LIT UP THE SKY, COST GROWERS A FORTUNE

In his relentless testimony, McWilliams recalled for the senators another blunder by the all-powerful monopoly that cost growers a fortune.

It was in 1993 when 'tombstone,' or fusarium head blight, first hit Red River Valley crops. This tombstone turns affected kernels dark, creates a mossy coating. The board acted as if it hadn't seen this disease before. Elevators refused to buy the grain. Many despairing farmers burned their crops in the field. The flames turned the sky red.

But tombstone strikes frequently in the US and the trade there has devised a simple sensible answer. It blends affected grain with good grain and uses it for regular baking purposes. So US elevators were buying. And at least one American grower cashed in on Canada's costly mistake.

A farmer from Langdon, ND, spotted this strange ritual of burning fields of valuable wheat, and he headed for Manitoba with his truck in October. He paid about $2.10 Cdn. (near the Wheat Board initial price) for no. 5 feed wheat. Back in North Dakota, he got about $4 for it, nearly doubling his money. This was too good to be true. He hired three more trucks and hauled all winter, making two trips most days. Rumour said **he made enough to retire.**

Some Canadian farmers took notice, began hauling grain across the border to get that $4. But many trucks were turned back by Canada Customs.

LACK OF FREEDOM COST $10,500 ON 3000 BU.

McWilliams related to the senators how his neighbour Ken McCannell also paid a heavy price for senseless board rules. McCannell grew a good durum crop in 1991. But the monopoly's quota restricted sales to five Bu. per acre. McCannell grew another good crop the next year but tiny quotas added to his carryover. By summer, 1993, his bins were still full. He would soon need space for his new crop.

His durum weighed a heavy 64 lbs. per Bu and graded 2CW. The nearby US price hovered around $5.60 per Bu. **But the Board's buy-back rules** stonewalled him from taking his grain there. He had no choice but to dump it as feed grain, accepting a no. 5. A producer car took it to Quebec, and he netted $2 per Bu. With the price difference $3.50 per Bu., McCannell's loss on the 3000 Bu. was $10,500, a cruel blow for a grower trying to pay his bills.

MONOPOLY FAVOURS LOCAL MALTING COMPANIES OVER GROWERS; TRUCKING BARLEY TO US SHOWS WHAT WE MISSED

McWilliams recalled for the senators how he began growing malting barley but again politics got in the way. Ottawa's monopoly system of selling prairie malting barley was set up about the time of the Second World War. And he said it has never properly accessed world markets to the farmers' benefit.

Rather, it seemed to favour Canada's malting companies, gave them first pick of the barley samples, and the chance to produce the world's best malt. But this did nothing for the farmer who produced good malting barley that wasn't accepted.

"Trucking barley to the US in recent years has shown us what we have been missing - that the world wants to buy our barley," he said. "Much of the barley we've trucked to the US gets resold to off-continent markets. And the US companies that paid big dollars re-sold it at a comfortable profit.

"So where was our Wheat Board all the while? And why weren't we capturing these markets?" He urged the Senate panel to ask many questions about malting barley.

FEED BARLEY GROWERS SUBSIDISE THE WORLD

McWilliams is convinced **feed** barley prices are also rigged against prairie growers by the government board. "All growers know Ottawa has manipulated our feed barley pricing policy to benefit poultry and livestock producers in other parts of Canada," he told the senators.

"This didn't worry us until now, because prairie barley was fed here and went south as beef or pork. But more recently, the Board has been pricing feed barley at lower and lower levels in relation to other grain. Presumably this benefits livestock farmers," he said.

McWilliams said that Wheat Board Chief Lorne Hehn admitted to the game being played when he addressed an Alberta town meeting during the barley vote debate. He told growers that barley exports must be restricted to meet domestic demands. Only then could sizeable exports be considered.

An exasperated McWilliams objected, "It is one thing

for prairie growers to have to subsidise Canadian consumers, as we've been doing. But our hog industry is now expanding fast, based on feed barley prices. So we growers will be subsidising consumers in every country that buys the pork."

And he asked, "Why do we want to hang the economics of a big hog industry on the necks of western barley growers? Why should we pay?"

The simple answer? "Sell feed barley on world markets, then the price will find its own level," he said. "Hog growers and barley growers will both benefit. When barley prices rise, growers will produce more. And the world pork price will find its own level."

VALUE-ADDED IS KEY - OATS, PASTA, MACARONI INDUSTRIES WAIT TO BE BORN

One over-riding truth haunts Canada's prairies today - value-added is the key to a prosperous satisfying future. McWilliams gave the senators some examples of how this works. A new Can Oat processing plant at Portage la Prairie removes the hulls from milling oats, slashing the oats' weight by 30 percent. This saves freight, and the hulls are fed to livestock in Manitoba. It creates jobs in the Can Oat plant and in trucking, and in meatpacking as well.

More important, it creates a new high value industry - a cash crop for farmers and a new income into Manitoba. And it increases the value of all prairie oats. In fact, other such plants are now being built.

"But remember," says McWilliams, "this new plant couldn't have been built under a wheat board monopoly. Thank goodness former Wheat Board Minister Charlie Mayer yanked oats from board control when he did. Companies must be able to pick and choose their quality of grain and their timing of purchase to suit their marketing strategy. They won't tolerate interference from bureaucrats."

Or look at pasta and macaroni, he added. These two flour products are begging to be produced in the prairies - an industry waiting to be born. North Dakota has 14 pasta plants, Manitoba doesn't have one. Yet good durum is grown in the southern prairies. If companies could by-pass the monopoly board and select grain according to their market strategy, they would locate here. But he said Manitoba will never have world class pasta plants while the monopoly is intact.

Yet Ottawa's monopoly board and the Liberal government directing it, oppose any move to value-added with just about every fibre of their being.

GROWERS SUBSIDISE POLITICS

McWilliams despaired of the present system. The board's sales policy fails to give the highest market value for the good wheat and durum, he said. And his insight goes back a long way. As a young man, he stayed on the family farm because he believed "Our wheat board was doing the ultimate to find the highest returns for us."

Now, it has been a shocker to learn what has really been going on. A few months ago he learned that Ottawa has purposely withheld grain sales many times since World War II for political or international reasons.

"We knew there was a backup in grain movement on those occasions, but we didn't know why," he told the senators. "I said to a well-known agricultural economist in January, 1997, that the most difficult years for me had been from 1968 to '73. We had only a five bushel quota each year from 1968 to 71. And 1972 was only 7 bushels."

The economist asked, "Do you know why that was?"

I answered "No."

"His response was shocking. Canada had entered the International Grains Agreement with the US and Australia to reduce sales and to see that each country sold the same amount. The idea was to not further depress world wheat and durum prices.

"But we growers had never been told," said Alex. "When we heard the term, 'International trade agreement,' we thought of a price cap. Now, years later, we learn it was a trade agreement which included selling only 5 bushels per specified acre."

He urged the senators, "We must never let these issues be kept secret from us ever again."

McWilliams addressed the senators with passion for good reason - this issue has been at the very heart of his own farm business and of his family life and his community, for decades. He had thrown himself into the struggle to support Andy McMechan who lives not far away.

"The Wheat Board and Customs threw unlimited funds into battling farmers," he says. And he knew the issue well enough to say, "Taxpayers would be outraged if they knew how their tax dollars were squandered.

"But the growers' pioneering spirit held strong in supporting McMechan and others. Farmers stuck together through the hundreds of court hearings, the strategy planning meetings, the costly telephone conference calls, and the work gangs. They continued helping each other with equipment and finance in amazing ways.

"Yes, they hoped they might get paid some day. But mostly they thought of this as the cost of eventually winning freedom for all growers and for their children who might one day farm."

"NOT THE WORK OF SELFISH MEN"

Recalled McWilliams, "My son and I experienced that 'togetherness' one late September day in 1996, when a work party was harvesting Andy McMechan's crop. Andy was serving jail time so he couldn't be present.

"Some crews were harvesting grain, others were setting up grain storage and bringing in and stacking hay. About 6.30 p.m., rain forced combines to shut down. Thirty men gathered for a big supper put together by wives.

"My son and I had been helping repair corrals to get ready for weaning time. As we drove home that evening, I thought, 'What I have seen today is not the work of selfish men.'"

MLA'S GET HUNDREDS OF CALLS FROM DESPERATE GROWERS; BANKS FORCED TO BY-PASS RULES

McWilliams was lunching with an MLA in the Manitoba legislature in 1997 and he suggested growers should have the option to bypass the Board and market any Board grain not sold by June 1st. They would then keep the money. The MLA's reply was startling.

"We MLA's get dozens of letters and hundreds of phone calls every April from farmers with the same problem," he said. McWilliams recalls, "A banker told me this is a major problem for banks too. Banking policy requires farmers to clean up last year's loans before setting up next year's line of credit. But the banker admitted, 'Sometimes we are forced to bypass banking rules so the farmer can plant his crop.'"

The problem is that in many years, most of the crop goes to market in June and July 10 or 11 months after it is harvested instead of in the fall months. But why this delay? McWilliams asked the Senate to investigate.

In this litany of failure, one question loomed ever larger in McWilliams' mind. How much longer could the politicians continue to brush off the increasing evidence that reform was long overdue?

A FREEDOM CRY!

McWilliams' closing words to the Senate Panel perhaps uttered the most important challenge facing Canada today. They were a freedom cry that went to the country's very heart. "The Western grain industry requires more freedom from the board monopoly than the proposed Bill C-4 allows," he cried. "Return the bill to the House of Commons with instructions to draft a new Bill. And that bill must include the rights of all grain producers.

"Those wanting to sell through the Board should be free to do so. Those wanting to market or export elsewhere should have the same freedom to choose."

But some senators were too busy asking questions about the business of feeding cattle and didn't seem to hear them.

MANITOBA ALSO PAID A BITTER PRICE

McWilliams' freedom cry echoed in another event in his province that occurred just before this book went to press. President Peter Holle of the Frontier Center for Public Policy shone a fresh light onto one vital part of that battle. He looked at Winnipeg which was once Canada's grain center as well as the largest grain exchange in the world. And he put that city's decline into a new perspective.

Peering back into history, he wrote that Winnipeg was the West's trading and commercial center at the end of the Second World War. It boasted many corporate headquarters. But when Ottawa gave the CWB a permanent marketing monopoly in 1943, "..it effectively shut down the city's vibrant grain exchange, then the world's largest.

"That move effectively drove out the critical entrepreneurial element, the spark of a dynamic economy. The board's absolute control over exports, together with freight subsidies for grain transport...(did it)."

And then, Holle noted, the introduction of dairy and poultry marketing boards across Canada in the 1970's, "..suffocated Winnipeg's (and Manitoba's) food processing industry.

"Minneapolis, once Winnipeg's size, zoomed ahead by leaving well enough alone."

14

STUDIES SCREAM OUT, "MONOPOLY A RELIC OF THE PAST...THAT IS WEAKENING THE WEST"

One of Canada's great myths was being debunked in 1998 and 1999 - not by shouting politicians, but by a parade of new studies shining fresh light on the shackled grain industry and the West.

NEW STUDIES REVEAL THE 'ADMINISTERED' GRAIN SYSTEM BANKRUPTS GROWERS, BLOCKS INVESTMENT, CHASES AWAY THE KIDS

Two prairie research economists might as well have screamed out, "Look, the Emperor has no clothes!" when they unleashed the findings of their new study in 1999. They had focused a blazing light on our rich and productive grain belt and on the hallowed system built up to exploit it. And in fact, on the prairies itself.

Dr. Graham Parsons and Dr. William Wilson noted that Canada and the US share the continent's spring and winter wheat and barley area - a fabulously fertile food belt that comprises much of our prairie provinces and the adjacent North Plains states of Montana, North and South Dakota and Minnesota. But they discerned a little understood phenomenon - the two countries have shaped entirely different systems in this breadbasket. And before they were done, Parsons/Wilson put that prairie treasure house into a long-overlooked and little understood perspective.

Canada's system is dominated and driven by politics. At its heart is the all-powerful monopoly wheat board which ranks among Canada's largest half dozen business organisations. This system was shaped by politicians. And our political elite have used it from the start to hold the west tight in its iron grip.

These researchers described Canada's grain industry as an 'administered' system where competition is a nasty word. They found that the government board's role is to sell virtually all the grain under its control. And in carrying out that mission, it sets up committees to allocate grain deliveries, storage capacity and railway cars. Ottawa also imposes cost-based rail prices and allocates how much grain each company can deliver and when.

That monopoly board even stands aloof from Canada's Competition Act. And this restricts the actions of every group that wants to improve the system. It's the bureaucratic way. And it entrenches old practices and shapes a system that is unable to meet today's challenges or prepare for challenges ahead.

The monopoly shapes almost every aspect of the prairies. The system it created and dominates has never been closely examined publicly. Yet every farmer must live with that creation, and many are now convinced that corruption thrives within it. No wonder it has become an unending political battleground.

Parsons/Wilson found that this bureaucratic system which virtually ignores market forces, is inevitably rife with inefficiencies. Government rather than business does much of the investing. It puts money into rehabilitating branch lines and into port storage. It buys 70% of the hopper cars.

And the system compares badly to the competitive system in the US. No wonder their findings have resonated across the West and through to Ottawa.

The US system is laden with incentives. Markets allocate resources, slashing handling costs and triggering extra services. This attracts massive investment in new technology to boost grain capacity. And it lowers handling, rail and port charges. Vessels at US ports wait only one-third the time to pick up grain as do ones at Vancouver.

Thanks to that competitive system, North Dakota has 260 grain handling (country elevation) companies. Saskatchewan has only 26. US elevators, whether on-farm, off-farm or at ports, are twice as big as those in Canada. And they provide more storage and capacity in the system to meet surge demands. The US also has more unit trains speeding grain to market and slashing costs.

1

Marketing costs have fallen steadily since the US deregulated its system back in 1980. Country elevation costs in ND are only half those in Saskatchewan. Terminal elevation costs are only one-third, and cleaning costs are only two-thirds of Saskatchewan's. And no handling fees are charged directly to US farmers.

The payoff for the entire US grain industry has been enormous. Every grower cashes in big time from competitive pricing. One recent study showed North Dakota's growers got $36.28 per tonne more for wheat than Saskatchewan growers and $45.31 more for barley. And because of the greater efficiencies in marketing, handling, and transportation, North Dakota and Montana growers were getting an extra $400-$500 million annually for their grain by 1995 and '96 compared to Saskatchewan growers.

Yet Parsons/Wilson found Canada's potential for competition is huge. Growers' average distance to an elevator on a competing railway is less than 50 km. compared to 187 km. in the US. But regulations here prevent growers and the trade cashing in.

"Scrap those regulations," they urge, and Canada's prairies could surge ahead once more.

These authors brought powerful credentials to their study. Dr. Parsons is President of Regina-based Organisation for Western Economic Co-operation. Dr. Wilson is an economist at North Dakota State University. And before they were done, they put that prairie treasure house into that long-overlooked perspective.

But astonishingly, their explosive study is only one of three new studies that are dramatically changing our perceptions of the West, and of Canada itself. And they come at a time when rock-bottom grain prices and rising costs have set the stage for massive change. They offer a path to a new future for this prairie resources treasure house.

CAN THE LOYNS/CARTER STUDY SAVE THE FARM?

Scientists Dr. Al Loyns and Dr. Colin Carter also looked deeply into these political events that are rocking the prairies and Canada itself. In their 1998 book, **A Study in Over-Regulation,** they went back to pioneer days and to the shining dream of the huge grain industry to be created. Yes, the politicians' mission then was to settle and develop this resources treasure-house so every Canadian could benefit. That is what Canada was about. The Wheat Boom era in the first three decades of this century brought remarkable prosperity as acreage was expanding and yields improving.

But now a deep discontent had come to the boil. Loyns/Carter found that when growers deliver grain to the monopoly board, they lose all say over how and when it will be stored, transported and marketed. And with competition gone, few incentives remain to cut costs. Growers take the huge losses.

They found Ottawa's grain monopoly controls over 75 percent of all prairie wheat and 30 percent of barley. It ranks among Canada's largest half dozen businesses in dollar sales. Yet at heart, it's not a business at all – it's a political structure. And it shapes the west in a way that is only now being understood.

These authors are not yokels trying to raise their media profile by making outrageous charges. They brought impressive credentials to their task. Loyns grew up in Manitoba, earned a PhD from the University of California, Berkeley. He taught and researched at the University of Manitoba from 1968 to 1998. He was Chief Economist for Dr. Beryl Plumtre when she headed Ottawa's high profile Food Prices Review Board. He received a Fulbright Research Award (1997) and was President of the Canadian Agricultural Economics Society (1996-97.) He is now President, Prairie Horizons. And he farms in Manitoba.

Carter grew up in Alberta and got his PhD in Agricultural Economics from University of California, Berkeley, in 1980. He is now Professor and Chair of Agricultural Resource Economics at the U. of California, Davis. He has received several research awards from professional associations for published research including a 1998 Distinguished Policy Contribution Award from the American Economic Assoc., for research on state trading organisations.

The two economists document an amazing story.

MONOPOLY SHAPES EVERY ASPECT OF PRAIRIE LIFE - BUT IT CAN'T WORK

They explain that Ottawa imposed the wheat monopoly in 1943, and extended it to barley and oats in 1949. Since then, that monopoly has been wielding a crushing impact on every aspect of prairie life. It shapes how every grain farmer runs his business and how he and his family and their neighbours live. It regulates how they deal with elevators and terminals on the grains it controls. It decides how and when they can deliver and get paid for their grain. So it determines their cash flow.

It even shapes the operations of cattle and hog and poultry men because feed grains are their major cost. And it determines how every grain company and just about every other prairie business operates. In fact, it has moulded our 'administered' prairie economy into one where freedom and competition and the market place are virtually unknown.

By probing deeply into this monopoly, the two scientists examined the prairies itself. And they came to one other astounding conclusion. Despite all the protests by monopoly spokesmen and by its political supporters, it has one fatal weakness. Single desk selling in world wheat and barley markets can't possibly work. It can't achieve the higher prices it claims to get. And for a simple reason. "Why would importers consistently pay the Board more than necessary?"

In fact, they found monopoly selling slashes buying competition, distorts price signals and prevents growers analysing the extra value they could get from more inputs. Resources are misallocated. Farmers and society pay.

A RELIC OF THE PAST, BUT A TOOL OF LIBERAL GOVERNMENTS

And they made one further momentous finding. Yes, any observer would assume this all-powerful monopoly is there because prairie people demand it. But not so! It is not a response to the informed demand of growers. No vote was held to get growers' wishes.

Now, most of Canada's commercial crown agencies have been privatised. But for the wheat board, time has passed it by. It's a relic of the past. Yet Ottawa continues to impose it on the West.

These researchers don't try to cloak their findings in euphemisms or soft talk. They found that despite growers' rising anger and an increasingly hostile environment, the Board has hardly changed for decades. Minister Goodale's attempt to shape a new CWB Act in 1998 proved a feeble effort.(i.e., The monopoly's Chief Executive Officer is still appointed by the Crown; directors must swear allegiance to maintaining the Board; and the Crown does not legally answer to farmers.)

No, the monopoly has become a creature of the Liberal party, which has largely governed Canada since the depression. And the Liberals use it as they see fit.

Loyns/Carter tell how politicians have been tightening the monopoly's stranglehold on growers over the decades. And discontent has been growing since the early 1970's. Angry growers formed the Palliser (now Western) Wheat Growers Association in the late 1960's to mount a furious challenge to it. They continue to fight for marketing choice and freedom.

But when livestock feeders in vote-rich Central Canada challenged Board pricing powers in a '69-'72 grain price crisis, Ottawa responded by throwing itself on side with these grain users. It freed up domestic feed grain marketing in 1974 and 1976, and kept the lid on exports so Ontario/Quebec feeders could get prairie grain at cheaper prices. And Central Canada's users benefited again when the Crow rates were modified by the Western Grain Transportation Act.

Now, hostility to the board is coming from the US where growers say its lower prices are undercutting their prices at home.

Lawmakers provide farmers across Canada with boards for particular reasons, say Loyns/Carter. When poultry and dairy farmers wanted to restrict production so they could set prices arbitrarily in the 1970's, they lobbied for supply management boards. Politicians responded. The boards came with lots of protection and benefits. They survived because producers managed regional coalitions in a national program.

DEFINITELY NOT A PRODUCER BOARD!

But the grain monopoly isn't a producer board. It originated in the Depression, was made compulsory in wartime. No producer votes have been held on CWB regulation. When a plebiscite was held on bringing canola into the monopoly, growers said "No!"

The monopoly had broad support in earlier years but **that has fallen dramatically.** Over 60 percent favoured free choice over compulsion in a 1995 Alberta vote on marketing barley. And a small grower sample in Saskatchewan polled similar results in early 1996. A few growers were recently elected to the board. But its legislated responsibility is still to carry out Ottawa's master plan. This puts elected directors in an impossible situation. Must they follow their legislated duty to serve only the board? Or can they fulfil their duty to serve the voters who elected them?

When Minister Goodale set up the **Western Grain Marketing Panel**, he chose its members to be strong Board supporters. But the pressure for change was so great in 1996 that panel members called for massive industry deregulation.

Ottawa's 1997 barley marketing plebiscite was an all-or-nothing vote on retaining the monopoly – not one to allow growers to simply opt out and sell their own grain if they chose. Yet 32 percent voted against retaining the board at all. They wanted freedom.

No, the Board isn't surviving on producer demand. Broad-based support has collapsed.

"THE MONOPOLY IS WEAKENING THE WEST" – SUPPORT FADES

Why would one political party be addicted to monopoly grain marketing? Loyns/Carter found that the Liberal government used the monopoly as part of the war effort from 1939-'45. Then it retained the board's compulsory powers in 1948 to meet Canada's commitments to Britain on post-war food supplies. It brought oats and barley under its monopoly in 1948, then made the board permanent in 1967. And it used that monopoly again in the 1970's to give feed grain users in central and eastern Canada their supplies of prairie grain at "corn competitive" prices.

The Liberals also used their Wheat Board-centred power to support the 1979 embargo on sales to Russia. And when world food security erupted as a political issue in the 1980's, the Liberals used Board power for credit sales to several countries, as well as for food aid to developing countries.

Yes, the monopoly is accountable only to Ottawa. It is often made an instrument of federal policy. And it conceals information on its transactions, making it easier for Ottawa to run these programs.

When a Conservative government yanked oats from the monopoly in 1989, sales to the US soared.

Loyns/Carter say the same Liberal forces that support the monopoly board subsidised grain shipments off the prairies. And that weakened the West by subsidising meat production and other food processing and job creation in the East.

Those Liberal forces still retain supply management in poultry and dairy to support the East at the expense of the West. And in revising the CWB Act in 1988, they retained the monopoly despite massive opposition, for a simple reason. It serves nicely as a state trader. And Liberal governments use it to wield food power at the negotiating table.

In contrast, the US uses Public Law 480 and the Commodity Credit Corporation for the food component of its foreign policy.

"OPEN THE BORDER TO THE PRIVATE TRADE"

Loyns/Carter also made the curious finding that 'lots of fiction' goes along with this system. Wheat Board and wheat pool consultants keep insisting the board has market power. They say more sales into the US would erode prices, hurting our growers. They even insist our farmers get higher returns because the Board 'looks after' this market.

But Loyns/Carter could find no evidence of this at all. Canada is a price-taker in the big US feed grain and malting market because it's a small supplier. And inefficiencies of single-desk barley selling to the US far outweigh any benefit.

They proposed a simple remedy. "Open the border to the private trade," they urged Ottawa. "Farmers would benefit enormously."

In fact an open border has already been tried with great success. Ottawa's Tory government ended Board control over US barley exports in its last days of power on Aug. 1, 1993. This opened a continental barley market. It lasted for only five weeks. Then a federal court judge ruled it was beyond Ottawa's powers. A newly elected Liberal government quickly ended it.

But in those 40 days, between 1/2 and 1 million metric tons of barley was sold to the US. The most the Board had previously sold in a whole year was 0.47 mmt. Economists estimated that a continental barley market could bring 3.5 mmt of barley exports a year. And our exports could increase to the Pacific NW and California where demand is strong.

With this overwhelming evidence before them, more

and more growers have made up their minds. They demand that Ottawa end the board's monopoly grip on wheat and barley. They want dual marketing so they can make their own choice whether to sell through the board or to sell their own grain.

Some growers still fear the board would be doomed if it had to compete. But Loyns/Carter found that Australia has successfully shifted from a monopoly agency to a dual marketing system. They say dual marketing would work here.

LIBERALS THE BUTT OF WESTERN JOKES

Media people are coming to this same conclusion. National newspaper columnists (and U. of Calgary professors) David Bercuson and Barry Cooper spelled it out in the National Post. "The Liberals have demonstrated a remarkable lack of respect for western Canadians...(treating them) like children who need to be protected from themselves and from the bogeyman of national fractionalization that haunts the consciousness of Ottawa mandarins."

They added, "Until the Liberals acknowledge Canada is a federation, that westerners do not see the country as an outpost of the St. Lawrence Valley and that their views matter, the Liberal task force will continue to be the butt of Western jokes."

They concluded, "That is not good for the country. It's not good for the West. And it's disastrous for the Liberal party."

15

ESTEY CRIES OUT, "FREE UP GROWERS TO BECOME FAMILY PROFIT CENTRES, NOT WARDS OF STATE." KROEGER LAYS OUT RECOVERY STRATEGY

Ottawa named Justice Estey to find out why the prairie grain system kept failing. He warned that his proposals "cry out" to all Canadians because "Prairie grain is vitally important to our economy." With compromise impossible, Kroeger laid out blueprint for change.

FREE UP EACH GROWER TO BECOME A FAMILY PROFIT CENTRE - ESTEY

Justice Willard Estey (ret.) couldn't have been more astounded when he delved into the political quagmire of the prairie grain system. The retired Supreme Court Chief Justice wrote in his 1998 report that the industry was in the midst of a revolution. Researchers were creating high yielding grains and new growing methods to boost incomes. And growers were adopting them. With "value added" through meat and processed grain products expanding fast, further massive changes were on the way. Yes, the future was rich with promise.

Estey's study seemed to represent a historic turning point for the faltering industry. Ottawa's Liberals had finally responded to the mounting pressure to find out why that system kept failing. Agriculture Minister Lyle Vanclief, Wheat Board Minister Ralph Goodale and Transport Minister David Collenette had asked Estey to find the reasons.

And to propose solutions.

Estey took the direct approach. He brushed off the monopoly board's claims to legitimacy, said farmers are kept in the dark about what happens to their grain, from freight rates to cleaning and all between. And while growers pay all those costs, he found the secretive board fought every proposal to let those growers see into these operations.

If growers are to remain competitive, he said, those costs of moving grain to export must be slashed and the benefits returned to them. Give each grower a chance to become a "family profit centre," he urged. Free him up to act like a businessman and not like a ward of the state. Because of the industry's size and importance, he said, his proposals 'cry out' to all Canadians.

GROWERS DESERT WHEAT, SWITCH TO CANOLA, OATS AND OTHER CROPS

Estey pinpointed the biggest trend in prairie grain today - the on-going switch from wheat to non-board grains like canola, oats, alfalfa hay, canary seed, lentils, and peas. He called it a desperate move by growers to escape the monopoly's intrusion into their farm businesses and to boost their incomes.

And he said it is transforming the prairies. Growers slashed wheat output by 28 percent to 19 million tonnes from 1991 to '96. At the same time, they were more than doubling canola output to 6.3 million tonnes. With canola averaging $420 a tonne and wheat $185 in 1997/'98, canola rivalled wheat in total value.

RETURN GROWERS' PROPERTY RIGHTS – ALLOW THEM MARKET INFORMATION

He found that Canada's Charter "does not protect economic liberty or property rights. A deliberate choice was made to exclude them..."

Now, after 56 years, the monopoly's power must be slashed, returning rights to growers. Limit the Board to being a regulator and administrator, he urged. And he called for sweeping changes in the CWB Act to save growers money and allow them financial gains.

Since farmers themselves carry all transportation/marketing costs, he said they must get timely market information. Yet the board fights fiercely to keep them in the dark about contract arrangements.

Estey found a world grain industry in dramatic change. The United Kingdom and Russia were no longer our biggest grain customers – both have become grain exporters. New efficiencies in rail line hauling are threatening the Seaway, and its fate hangs on developing grain markets in the North and South Atlantic regions.

(A cynic might suggest that most people and businesses along the seaway have a vested interest in keeping the monopoly intact.)

When Estey looked at the underused financially troubled Port of Prince Rupert, he called for studies to identify its potential for more efficiencies and greater use. He found the sale of the Port of Churchill rail line and terminal to OmniTRAX, to be hopeful. For OmniTRAX operates short line railways in the US and Canada. And it has the potential to cut shipping costs and put an extra $6.25 million a year into farmers' pockets.

He called for more grain cleaning within the prairies to slash the costs of hauling dockage and to relieve port congestion. And he said farmers must retain the right to order and load producer cars.

Estey also called for change in the way farmers, grain companies and the board interact in moving grain to market. Put growers in the same position with Board grain as they are now with non-board grain which they sell themselves to the highest bidder. And they would reap the benefit.

He scoffed at the monopoly's proposal to seize power over all aspects of grain handling, called it self-serving. And he praised CP Rail's offer to pass on cost savings of up to $40 million per year in exchange for some deregulation. In fact, he urged Ottawa to end its control over grain movement.

"Focus on cost cutting," was his constant theme. Force railroads, including short line ones, to compete so farmers can get better service. And he called on Ottawa and the provinces to apply part of the fuel taxes to the municipal grid road system and secondary provincial highways.

He also urged Ottawa to abandon rail branch lines, and to replace old wooden elevators with high throughput ones. For these new terminals along with unit trains are transforming the industry with their huge efficiencies. And he said large truck transport is hauling efficiently from farms to distant large-scale elevators.

PARE BACK THE BOARD'S ROLE

Despite the breathtaking changes transforming the industry, the Justice had been startled to find the monopoly board simply doles out grain to companies based on their historic market share. This left no incentives to boost efficiency and no way to pass the savings along to farmers.

Estey didn't say it, but that grain is the cash cow for those grain companies, so they are likely to be compliant to the monopoly.

Pare back the board's role to sales and marketing, he urged Ottawa. Allow it "no operations or commercial role" in handling/transportation. And let farmers decide when and how their grain moves to market.

He urged Ottawa to make the monopoly sell grain direct to grain companies, forcing these firms to bid for it, rather than the board simply doling it out on a market share basis. Grain companies would then force railways to bid at auction on shipping it. The savings would go back to growers.

In calling for an end to the freight rates cap, he urged, "Don't ship any grain until it is sold."

HARD-NOSED REPORTER PULLS NO PUNCHES-THE MUDDLED MANDATE

George Koch is one reporter who doesn't go for easy euphemisms when tough issues are being discussed. And in a National Post column, this seasoned prairie grain journalist went to the very guts of Estey's report. The wheat board's mandate is so muddled, he wrote, its relations with grain companies so cosy - judging by the interchange of senior officials including the wheat board's new president, a former pool executive, - the two sometimes appear indistinguishable.

Those prophetic words proved only too accurate in 1999 when former Wheat Board Commissioner Rick Klaasen signed on with Saskatchewan Wheat Pool. Farm leaders quickly charged that he failed to wait the required 2 years after leaving the Board so he could not bring board secrets to the grain company employing him.

Koch saw the monopoly board's job in simple terms. It's to sell almost all board grains to buyers inside and outside Canada. And also to administer Ottawa's programs to support farmers. And he said Estey's focus on the "socialized, regulated, secretive and paternalistic world of Prairie grain farming," would be considered "subversive and even revolutionary" by some groups. But he couldn't disagree more.

He called Estey an impartial third party who "discarded the board's claim to legitimacy." Koch described the monopoly's secret "Marxist world," and he called groups like the National Farmers Union, the Prairie wheat pools, and Saskatchewan's NDP the board's 'inferior officers' or acolytes. But he predicted Estey's report will sweep into them like a Prairie dust storm.

Koch said the board "lies" when it tells farmers its "single-desk selling system gives it 'market power' – a cartel-like ability to elevate world grain prices," that benefits farmers. And he praised Estey's proposal that gains from changes to the wheat board must actually find their way to farmers.

"In the tortured world of prairie grain handling, such an equitable division is by no means assured," he said.

THAT SHATTERED MYTH – "POLITICIANS CAN SELL THE PRAIRIE GRAIN CROP"

Yes, these three studies by Parsons/Wilson, by Loyns/Carter and by Estey, left no room for doubt. A great Canadian myth had been shattered – the one that said a government monopoly with its politicians and armies of bureaucrats could sell the huge prairie grain crop at higher prices than traders or growers themselves could get. And it could return more money to growers and lead the way to shaping stronger communities and a stronger country.

Prairie folk learned that myth before they ever hit kindergarten. It was rooted in the 'social gospel' which in pioneer days had pronounced capitalism the evil enemy. And it deeply permeated prairie culture - and indeed much of Canada's. It became almost a religious-based faith in much of the West. To question it was to invite the wrath of Canada's powerful left wing political establishment, which ruled for decades, and in fact, rules much of the west and Canada even today.

Yet the truth is that the West is now hurting badly, falling futher and further behind its vast potential.

Only one question remains. How soon can our politicians face up to the truth and set the monopoly aside. If the West and Canada are to be saved, growers and the industry must be freed. Every day freedom is denied further imperils the country.

Estey concluded his report with the ringing words, "Prairie grain is vitally important to our economy." But implementing that report would be a massive undertaking.

KROEGER AIMS TO BRING FACTIONS TOGETHER

Faced with this critical need to bring efficiency back into the system, Transport Minister David Collenette acted. He named prestigious consultant Dr. Arthur Kroeger as Grain Handling and Transportation Facilitator, assigned him the job of bringing the railways, grain companies and growers together around the table to seek a concensus on how to achieve Estey's goals. The challenge was to get desperately needed revenue back to growers and others in the system.

Kroeger launched a series of intense meetings. And Wawota, Sask., grower Keith Lewis was part of that working group. He emerged from those meetings full of pessimism. And he explained later that it turned out to be impossible to bring the various groups together onto common ground. After so many years in a tightly regulated political system, the differences between various farm groups were not about to give. Nor were the entrenched views of the grain companies and the railroads. The meetings were full of violent disagreement.

"Those industry players get their pay cheques from the system," said Lewis. "So its not surprising they should ask why should they take the risk of going to a competitive open market system? Under the wheat board monopoly, the risk is all passed back to the farmers.

"In fact," he said, "those discussions showed the issue of breaking the wheat board's power and control over the industry could not be resolved through negotiation. The discussions accomplished little."

Lewis looked at the broader picture. "We now have a tremendous farm crisis in the West, - the worst in anyone's memory. And we can't find a way out of it. What disturbed me was the inability of grain companies to think outside their short term corporate interests. At no time did they indicate they were ready to crawl out from behind the skirts of mother wheat board."

Lewis is convinced the prairie grain industry is unable to fully respond to this crisis. "We lack the people. The capital is not here. And the political will is not here to meet this challenge."

When the discussions accomplished little, Kroeger had no choice but to write his own report. He handed it, along with his recommendations, to Mr. Collenette in September, '99.

He endorsed the vital issue of the Board buying the grain from the farmer rather than simply seizing it. And he recommended that the Board purchase 25% of its grain from grain companies in the first year, 50% the second, and 75% the third. If the results were good, the move would continue to 100%.

He called on the Board, as an export agency, not to take custody of the grain until it is loaded on board a ship. And when grain companies gain revenue from blending grain, growers should be paid for it.

Give grain companies maximum scope to compete for growers' grain, he urged, by adjusting the various charges for moving grain from the farm to ship. Also, make grain companies pay interest and storage charges on grain as an incentive to get it on board the ship quickly, efficiently.

Kroeger also called for a cap on the railways' grain handling revenues. And reduce this cap gradually through rate reductions to be certain railroads kept improving their efficiencies, he urged. In fact, force the railways to compete more vigorously, bringing down costs.

He said the Wheat Board's central role in grain transportation must be replaced with new competitive arrangements. And he assured Mr. Collenette that such a market-based system would benefit growers greatly.

16

TOUGH-TALKING P.M. TELLS UKRAINE, "MONOPOLIES A RECIPE FOR POVERTY, STAGNATION."

But Chretien kept jailing his own prairie growers who tried to take his advice and sell their own wheat and barley. Is this part of the hidden agenda of Ottawa's Liberals to control the West for their own purposes?

P.M. ATTACKS UKRAINE'S MONOPOLIES! WHY NOT OURS?

Prime Minister Jean Chretien travelled to the Ukraine in early 1999, and at one event in this former Soviet state, he cast caution aside. In addressing University students, he tried tough talk and perhaps statesmanship. And he offered advice from the heart.

He warned these future leaders that if the Ukraine doesn't get rid of its "monopolies," it faced "poverty and stagnation."

In fact, he said, "Monopolies are not worthy of a great nation and a great people." He even pledged Canada's support for those people in their "much delayed transition into a market economy." But he stated the Ukraine "must create a new class of honest entrepreneurs to break from its Communist legacy."

In delivering that ringing challenge, Mr. Chretien seemed to forget he had media along. And when his remarks were reported back home in Canada's prairies, many growers went into a state of near shock. After all, many were in financial crisis. And study after study had shown Ottawa's own all-powerful grain monopoly bears much of the blame. For it denies growers their freedom to sell their own crops and to process them. And in fact, to manage their own industry.

When Mr. Chretien's remarks in the Ukraine were reported, every Canadian should have cried out in response, "What's that again? Hasn't the Prime Minister noticed that Canada's prairies are similarly trapped in an all-powerful monopoly?"

One could ask, "Hasn't the prime minister noticed that Saskatchewan, which is hit hardest by the Ottawa monopoly, is suffering much like the Ukraine? Its population has stagnated at about 1 million for 60 years. And Manitoba's growth has been similarly blocked."

CHRETIEN'S "POVERTY, STAGNATION AND ALIENATION" GOES BACK TO SOCIAL GOSPEL

In the prairies, Alberta alone has escaped the worst effects of that monopoly. That province's entrepreneurial people rejected the social gospellers' attack on capitalism and personal freedom from the start, focused on opportunities beyond selling wheat. And they have been creating jobs and wealth furiously. Alberta's soaring population has surpassed 3 million.

Chretien must have got carried away when he urged the Ukraine leaders to continue "..navigating the difficult passage from a command economy to a market economy." He even assured its future leaders that if the Ukraine continues "..the path towards economic reform and transition...the people of Canada will travel that path with you."

But on his return to Canada, he seemed to forget the message he preached there. Reform MP Garry Breitkreuz summed it up in the House of Commons, "I agree...that monopolies are a recipe for poverty and stagnation. But why are they bad for the Ukraine and good for Canada?"

He added, "The government will even put a farmer in handcuffs and leg-irons and take him away to jail for selling his own grain."

Why did Mr. Chretien cry out his message to the Ukrainian people and then turn his back on that message when he returned to Canada? Back in Ottawa, why didn't he step forward and tell this story to his cabinet, and insist that Mr. Goodale shut down the Board's propaganda machine and end the government monopoly?

"ORWELL'S WORLD WAS NOT TO BE..."

In an early New Year's 2000 column, the Calgary Sun's Paul Jackson shone a blazing light on the most pressing issue of the past century. Looking back, he recalled that the century began with socialists and their fellow travelers shouting from every rooftop that they would reshape the world. And "..by force and imprisonment of their opponents if necessary."

He wrote, "How the world won out against the adherents of Karl Marx, Adolf Hitler, Josef Stalin and the fraudulently-named 'social democratic' movements, is akin to an edge-of-the-seat thriller." These 'leaders' set out to create "..a utopian world in which capitalism and wars would be eradicated and benevolent governments would look after all our needs."

Then in the 1940's and 1950's, we Canadians had the 'social democrats' "..including T.C. Douglas – still propagandizing their beliefs and absolutely convinced capitalism was failing."

But, "Unbeknownst to them, the golden age of economic freedom described by Adam Smith in 1777 – and explained by the likes of Ayn Rand, Milton Friedman, Ludwig von Mises and Friedrich Hayek - was already taking shape."

Meanwhile, wrote Jackson, "Apologists for Moscow and its eastern European slave states – including Canada's New Democrats and to a degree Pierre Trudeau - never even had an inkling the world was to do a somersault...

"When the Berlin Wall fell with a resounding crash, it took the Soviet Union with it and socialism went into the garbage can.... The left had brought not peace, but war, and not security, but impoverishment....

"Not only was the left drastically wrong in its economic philosophy, but its tolerance for evil in the form of Marxism, and its intolerance for individuals and their rights, doomed it for disdain once the average wage-earner could plonk down the dollars for big-screen television.

"George Orwell's world was not, after all, to be the world of the 20th century. The much dreaded 1984 never came to pass."

Jackson believes the world has been saved from this cruel fate.

The story told in this book, much of it for the first time, is simply a small part of the world struggle Jackson describes. These growers wanted the freedom to sell their own wheat and barley to the highest bidder. They wanted the freedom to manage their own farms as business enterprises. They even wanted the freedom to get their grain processed in their home communities, creating value-added and jobs and wealth for their families and neighbors.

Yet they were caught up in this age-old freedom struggle. And this story has detailed some of the massive costs growers and the prairies and Canada itself have paid because of this lack of freedom.

If it is true that every generation must fight for its own freedom, no group has had a harder fight than these growers. For their battle has been against the awesome and relentless power of Ottawa's politicians and bureaucrats.

A NEW ERA DAWNS

As this book goes to press, further momentous events are shaking Canada. The ages-old duopoly of the Canadian National/Canadian Pacific railways hauling Canadian goods east and west and discouraging the movement north and south, is collapsing. CN's Chief Executive Paul Tellier pinpointed the issue clearly as his firm launched its initiative to team up with Texas-based Burlington Northern Santa Fe railway.

"North South traffic is the key to Canadian prosperity," he explained. And while this initiative was at least temporarily derailed by political action in the US, no one can doubt the truth of Tellier's statement.

Collapse of the Air Canada/Canadian Airlines duopoly sends out the same signal. And the death of Eaton's in the face of giants Wal-Mart, Home Depot and other US superstores, signals further massive change for Canada.

That old dream of a self-contained and socialist Canada from sea to shining sea has crumbled. Canada's days of hiding from world competition are fast ending. The people's standard of living will be linked directly to the amount of freedom they can win from government. And one thing is certain - the people will not be denied.

17

CONCLUSION

THAT MASSIVE WASTED OPPORTUNITY – THE PRAIRIE GRAIN INDUSTRY

OTTAWA'S MONOPOLY CONDEMNS GROWERS, INDUSTRY, TO BLEAK FUTURE

The tales of courage told in this book make it perhaps an unprecedented story. Thousands of growers, in their struggle to win freedom from the iron grip of Canada's biggest monopoly, received massive media coverage. They have been filmed as their trucks were seized and they were arrested and shackled and hauled off to jail. Their fierce battles have screamed out from TV screens, been reported in newspapers and have resonated on radio across the country. Millions of TV viewers have seen them jammed into courts fighting for justice.

In fact, they shined a blazing light into the politics of the huge prairie grain industry. And they found Ottawa's all-powerful grain monopoly guilty of arrogance and inefficiency, perhaps even of conflict of interest and of rigging the system. The cost to farmers, the West, and to Canada itself has been staggering.

But who are these remarkable people? What are their motives? Are they really criminals? Or are they a new generation of heroes?

This glimpse into Canada's very soul leaves no doubt. These growers are leading citizens respected and loved by neighbors and friends. Their simple goal is to somehow break the chains of Ottawa's monopoly that shackle them and their neighbors and deny them their freedom to manage their farm businesses. For their trouble, they are being vilified, fined and jailed by a government which has sadly forgotten its role is to serve the people rather than to control them. Many are risking everything in their freedom struggle.

And they are giving Canadians a long-denied insight into Ottawa's unrelenting obsession with controlling the West rather than freeing it up as a full partner in Confederation.

In this strange tale, Ottawa's grain monopoly emerges as the central tool by which these politicians exert their relentless control. That monopoly is one of Canada's biggest businesses. And its chains are exacting a terrible toll - destroying the farms and the home communities of numberless prairie citizens.

When these growers pulled back the curtain on these events, they found the monopoly is rife with arrogance. In one breathtaking display, a senior employee growled at growers who pay his wage, "If you don't like our selling system, go to the US."

Growers were shocked to discover that clandestine Wheat Board/Pool meetings have been held to quietly pass out 'inside' information to selected growers while denying it to others. And they asked, Was this an improper bid to rig the system?

When Prime Minister Chretien visited the Ukraine in early 1999, he offered students there some heart-felt wisdom. To build their country, he urged, they must get rid of their monopolies. His reason? "Monopolies are a recipe for poverty and stagnation."

But on his return to Canada, where the grip of Ottawa's own monopoly was never tighter, his sense of justice deserted him. He turned his back on the path he urged on the Ukraine, and refused to free up prairie farmers to manage their own farms and help lead their communities to greater wealth creation.

DOES MONOPOLY SELLING REEK WITH CONFLICT OF INTEREST?

Saskatchewan grower Carol Husband's endless searching uncovered still another daunting question. Does Ottawa's monopoly selling reek with conflict of interest? When Ottawa seizes the farmers' grain, it often directs it through the elevator terminals and the ships along the Great Lakes. And influential and well-connected Liberals are obvious beneficiaries of these policies.

Manitoba grower Alex McWilliams' own experience and his deep digging convinced him Ottawa's monopoly rigs both malting barley and feed barley prices. And he told a Senate committee, "Taxpayers would be outraged if they knew how their tax dollars were squandered as the Wheat Board and Customs threw unlimited funds into battling farmers."

Looking back at that freedom struggle, McWilliams noted, "The growers' pioneering spirit held strong in supporting McMechan and others. They stuck together through the hundreds of court hearings, the strategy planning meetings, the costly telephone conference calls, and the work gangs. They continued helping each other with equipment and finance in amazing ways."

DAVID BRYAN REFUSED TO BUCKLE TO OTTAWA'S TYRANNY

When Saskatchewan grower David Bryan refused to buckle to Ottawa's tyranny, and instead set out on his lonely high profile border crossing to sell his grain at higher world prices than he would get from the monopoly, his fate was sealed. He was seized, handcuffed, shown into the rear seat of a cruiser, read his rights, and driven to the RCMP detachment at Estevan. It was his first experience in handcuffs. And he later remembered vividly the discomfort. "I couldn't scratch if I got an itch."

To battle Ottawa's power to seize his grain, Bryan came back with his Charter Challenge on property rights and in doing it seemed to be taking on Ottawa's total might.

President David Somerville of the high profile National Citizen's Coalition exploded in anger at Ottawa's ongoing attack on grower Andy McMechan. "The Chretien government is persecuting the innocent while protecting criminals," he said. "It's no wonder freedom-loving farmers across Western Canada are outraged. In a society that prides itself as being free and democratic, it's frightening that farmers can be jailed for selling their own grain to the highest bidder. It's morally wrong. And its unconstitutional."

Somerville's Coalition acted, throwing its financial support behind McMechan and his struggle.

GROWERS DON'T OWN THE GRAIN THEY GROW

When Peace River, AB, farmer Bill Blake's research led him to the Encyclopaedia, he was shocked to find its definition of fascism seemed to come close to defining the Ottawa monopoly's operations and power.

And when one judge ruled that property rights are not protected in Canada's Constitution, astonished growers dug deeper and found property rights have never been written into Canada's Charter. Ottawa had been seizing prairie growers' grain for decades, flagrantly denying them the freedom they believed should be a right of every citizen in a free country – to sell their own produce in the open market to the highest bidder. And it denied them the freedom to manage their own farm businesses.

The message to every Canadian was clear. Ottawa can seize your automobile, your bank account, your RRSP, without a second thought. Yet further digging by these desperate growers revealed another strange truth. While prairie wheat and barley growers don't own the grain they grow and harvest, foreigners do get strong property rights in Canada.

The actions of these growers at a time when wheat and barley prices have been at disaster levels, have left no doubt – their farm communities are in crisis. The way to create more wealth and jobs and to save those communities and perhaps Canada itself is no mystery. A massive move to value-added - to converting that grain into processed food right at home in the prairies – is long overdue.

Yet Ottawa's monopoly largely denies growers and others the freedom to set up wheat and barley processing plants in the prairies. In fact its actions prevent the West from utilising its huge resources base to create wealth and help lead Canada into the future. That monopoly throws its vast power into preserving the past, denies the West its destiny.

Wheat Board Minister Ralph Goodale fairly screamed out Ottawa's arrogant and obsolete view of prairie farmers when he said they are unable to manage their industry themselves and Ottawa must do it for them.

A WORLD IN BREATH-TAKING CHANGE

Yes, in an earlier day, many world governments thought their job was to control their country's economy and the people themselves. But today's world is in breath-taking change. An industrial revolution has given way to a world revolution. A knowledge economy prevails. Countries lacking people with knowledge simply won't be able to compete in the world economy.

Today, the job of any legitimate government must be to help every person become full contributing members of society. It must free them and help them build their lives and the new economy, not shackle them and deny them opportunities.

The Regina Chamber of Commerce set out in late 1999 on a vital mission - a province-wide series of meetings asking the people to help devise a strategy for Saskatchewan's economy. Alberta's leaders had done this decades earlier, thus setting that province on its path of economic growth, low taxes, and value added.

Retired Saskatchewan Government official Bryce Baron put that into a stunning perspective. "Endless opportunities have passed (Saskatchewan) by over the years," he wrote in a newspaper column in November, '99. But in contrast, Alberta's deliberate and focused economic development strategy for at least 35 years has targeted three areas - petrochemicals, advanced technology and agricultural processing.

And Alberta's programs to develop these sectors have had breathtaking success. Its economy is now so widely diversified it hardly noticed recent low oil prices. Baron urged the Saskatchewan government to join the Chamber of Commerce and others in an all-party commission to implement a similar long-term strategy.

Further insights came from Prairie V.P. Dan Kelly of the Canadian Federation of Independent Business who said Alberta's low tax rates and surging economy were creating a brain drain from neighbouring provinces. And while the public has hardly noticed as legions of Manitobans and Saskatchewanites moved there, he said that will change as low grain prices squeeze these two provinces.

INDIVIDUAL LIBERTY, RESPONSIBILITY AND OPPORTUNITY

Distinguished Canadian scientist/philosopher Dr. WD Morrison focused on this freedom issue as few others have in recent years. Addressing the Ontario Institute of

Agrologists' 1993 annual meeting, he said, "Only a free individual can respond well to an opportunity....and if laws, red tape, protectionism and the like cumber one, a strong response to opportunity will be lacking."

Canadians are being "lawed" to death, with hiring laws, rent laws, pension laws and so on, he said. And Canada is subverting individual freedom (and individual responsibility) on every side, to the will of the State – and even if the majority wish it, it doesn't make it right or proper. Freedom of thought, association, trade and control or disposition of property should not be taken away.

Democracy and freedom are different, said Morrison. Democracy relates to the right to vote on a given matter. Freedom relates to a person's involvement with others or things in the private sector. Freedom to own property is a fundamental need in a true democracy. Private property implies a need for self-discipline, planning, saving, investing and economic security. We must never trade liberty for the promise of security.

HOW CAN GOVERNMENTS REMOVE PROPERTY RIGHTS FROM INDIVIDUALS FOR THE 'GOOD' OF THE MAJORITY?

It is frightening, said Morrison, that not one of the eleven political leaders in Canada then saw anything wrong with not having property rights enshrined in the proposed Constitution; indeed, that freedom was deliberately excluded. He recalled a statement made by Cicero, as quoted by Will Durant, "Often the leader in a democracy is someone bold and unscrupulous...who curries favor with the people by giving them other men's property."

We have fallen into the habit of allowing government.....to remove property from individuals for the "good" of the majority or society in general, he said

Philosopher H.L. Mencken stated some people believe "happiness is something to be got by taking it away from the other fellow," said Morrison. And Morrison added, "Once you admit that the individual is merely a means to serve the ends of the higher entity called society or the nation, most of the features of totalitarian regimes which horrify us follow of necessity.......Intolerance and brutal suppression of dissent, the complete disregard of the life and happiness of the individual, are essential and unavoidable consequences of this basic premise."

"Personal freedom," said Morrison, "is the freedom to do as I wish, so long as I do not infringe on another's freedom...Suppose I wish to paint graffiti on my house. I should be free to do so, but I am not free to do so on my neighbor's house. He or she has property rights."

ONLY FREE INDIVIDUALS CAN SEIZE OPPORTUNITY!

Freedom of the individual is an absolute requirement if we are to be open to opportunity, he said....Taking advantage of the opportunities in agriculture will require individual freedom. The history of discovery clearly shows the individual, not the group, is the key.

PLACE THE STATE'S WELFARE FIRST, AND CREATIVITY IS LOST

Compare countries where individuals are sacrificed for the welfare of the state, to even the semi-freedom enjoyed in Western cultures, he said. What great discoveries arose in the former Soviet Union or China in the last 50-60 years for the benefit of mankind? Compare food production, medicine, transport, care of the environment in the "free" countries to that where "wise governments" exercised control

Disraeli said, "Change is inevitable. In a progressive country, change is constant."

"GUARD INDIVIDUAL FREEDOM WITH UTMOST ZEAL"

We must guard freedom with the utmost zeal, said Morrison. It is the cornerstone and foundation of a free society. The individual's freedom as a consumer acts as the driving force for a capitalistic society. The consumer determines what product will sell and what product will not sell, rather than the one who makes the products. And it is the freedom of the one who makes the product to change it, which allows demand to increase.

GOVERNMENT'S ROLE – "ENSURE LIBERTY, NOT SLAVERY"

What then, is to be the role of government? Not to subjugate the individual for the welfare of the state, said Morrison, but rather to provide **protection, not provision,** to **ensure liberty, not slavery, to** ensure **peace, not strife**. Government intervention in other areas leads to more intervention, and special privilege leads to arbitrary law.

Thomas Jefferson said, "A wise and frugal government, which shall restrain men from injuring one another, shall leave them otherwise free to regulate their own pursuits of industry and improvement and shall not take from the mouth of labor, the bread it has earned."

Businesses which lose the competitive edge can change their product or service, can exit the market or petition the state to protect them. We have seen what happens when a group as massive as the European Economic Community decides to protect its agricultural industry from outside competition, by government intervention. This..... has had drastic influence on the agricultural industry in Canada because...we are in an international scene and we must survive there. The distinction between what is foreign and what is domestic becomes less and less clear and will continue to do so.

Morrison added, "...A tariff is a decree...forgiving an industry for all its economic sins, incompetence, mismanagement, lethargy and contempt for the customer."

Benjamin Franklin said, "They that give up essential liberty to gain a little temporary safety deserve neither liberty nor safety."

Morrison concluded with a quote, which related to the founding of the United States, but was equally true of Canada. "Let us dedicate ourselves to a renewed application of the ideal of individual freedom and individual responsibility, which (the) Pilgrim (fathers) learned at such sacrifice and which they passed on (to us) as (our) most precious heritage."

(Dr. Morrison was born in 1927 in Provost, Alta., where his Christian parents homesteaded He graduated from the University of Toronto in Agricultural Science, got his Ph.D. from the U. of Illinois in 1955. He was Director of Research for Maple Leaf Mills from 1955-1971, Prof. and Chair, Dept. of Animal and Poultry Science, U. of Guelph, 1971-82. He was a director of Yonge St. Mission, the Shanyman's Christian Assoc., the Canadian Scientific and Christian Affiliation and Heritage Baptist Seminary, a deacon of Kenmuir Baptist Church, Mississauga, and Crestwicke Baptist Church, Guelph. Honors in his professional life included the Golden Award, Canadian Feed Industry Assoc.; Fellow, Agricultural Institute of Canada; Award of Merit, Canadian Soc. Of Animal Science; Centennial Award, Ontario Ministry of Agriculture and Food; Award of Merit, Ontario Poultry Council; and Distinguished Agrologist Award, Ont. Inst. Of Agrologists. He died in early 2000.)

PRAIRIE GRAIN INDUSTRY IS A WASTED OPPORTUNITY

President Neil McMillan of the Saskatchewan gold mining firm Claude Resources, powerfully voiced his concern in the early days of the struggle, saying the monopoly board is unresponsive to changing needs and opportunities because it is a government bureaucracy. He called the board, "critically deficient" in helping farmers access international markets. And he accused the monopoly of leaving the province with a "strategically developed inferiority complex promoted aggressively by our politicians."

McMillan saw grain growers as businessmen. And he said, "Today's successful business sector requires five things, - identified international markets, the knowledge and technology to continually add value to its product, skilled labour capable of using modern technology to add value, capital to finance its operations, and a globally competitive management."

But growers "..have no control over their marketing agency." He estimated that, "..85% of the Canadian wheat shipped overseas represents wasted opportunities in value-added and niche marketing." As a result, Saskatchewan farmers represent 58,000 businessmen "who have deferred their most critical responsibility to government."

The stories in this book confirm McMillan's appraisal. Prairie grain is a wasted opportunity. The country's future depends on ending this catastrophe, and setting course for a new day.

Michael Interisano www.miphotography.com

About The Author

Ottawa-born Don Baron went into farm journalism following his graduation from Ontario Agricultural College in 1949. He joined the editorial staff of the western magazine Country Guide in 1952 and was named its first eastern field editor when it became a national publication in 1955. He was appointed editor in 1963, working out of Winnipeg.

He was named Head, Agriculture and Resources Broadcasting for CBC TV, in 1975, working out of Toronto. His producers filmed across Canada and beyond, bringing food and resources programming to the very centre of the network's schedule and winning some of the largest audiences ever achieved by this CBC division. Don was appointed Executive Director of the groundbreaking farmers' commodity group, Palliser Wheat Grower's Association, in 1979. He served from 1983 to 1990 as speech-writer for Premier Grant Devine in Saskatchewan and as Chief of Staff for Hon. Joan Duncan.

Baron was elected President, Agricultural Institute of Canada, in 1974, and President, Canadian Farm Writers' Federation. He was named a Commissioner of Enquiry into Vegetable Marketing in Manitoba, and a member of Manitoba's Commission on Targets for Economic Development. His writing has appeared in Maclean's, Toronto Star and other publications.

Don has written three earlier books. **CANADA'S GREAT GRAIN ROBBERY,** published in 1997, told the little known story of how American pastors a century ago, with their new Social Gospel message, targeted capitalism as the source of all evil, and aimed to turn over power to "trustworthy politicians" to make decisions for society. This idea was rejected by Americans but was welcomed by a few Canadian pastors and by many politicians at what can now be seen was at great cost to this country. **BATTLEGROUND,** (co-authored with Calgary Sun columnist Paul Jackson) tells the story of the Grant Devine Saskatchewan government from 1982 to 1991. **BEYOND ROGUES' HARBOUR** relates the epic tale of an Anglo-Canadian pioneer family tracing its roots from Ireland, Scotland and England. These people, (some of Don's ancestors among them) homesteaded first in the Ottawa Valley, then in Western Ontario, and then in the West.

If you wish to inquire about bulk book purchase orders or if you are interested in contacting Don for interviews or speaking engagements, he can be reached at Don Baron, 14 Wood Cr., Regina, Sask. S4S 6J7, Phone: 306-586-4578